The Metrop

M A C Horne

Capital Transport

First published 2003

ISBN 185414 275 5

Published in association with London's Transport Museum
by Capital Transport Publishing, 38 Long Elmes, Harrow Weald, Middlesex

Printed by CS Graphics, Singapore

The front cover painting is by Peter Green, GRA

The maps on pages 13 and 38 are by Mike Harris

CONTENTS

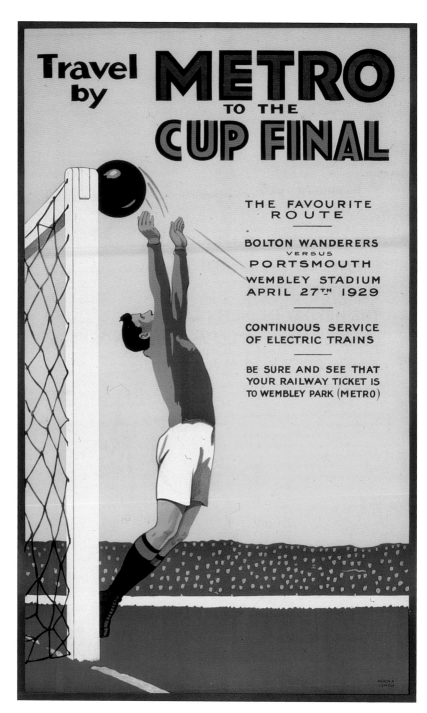

Metropolitan Railway poster for the 1929 FA Cup Final. LT Museum

The Metropolitan Railway

The name 'Metropolitan Line' was one of several adopted in July 1933 by the newly formed London Passenger Transport Board. At that time line names tended to reflect historical ownership, so it is no surprise to find the name 'Metropolitan Line' representing the bulk of the services hitherto operated by the newly-defunct Metropolitan Railway. The unwieldy Metropolitan Line title then covered more services than it does today, including the service from Hammersmith (and Addison Road) to Whitechapel (later Barking) that is now part of the Hammersmith & City Line and falls outside the scope of this book. What we are concerned with here are the origins of the present services from Baker Street to the north-west.

The Metropolitan Railway (Met) opened for business on 10th January 1863, operating steam-hauled trains between termini at what are now called Paddington and Farringdon but were then Bishops Road and Farringdon Street. This new railway was devised to help reduce endemic traffic congestion, the narrow streets being cluttered up with slow-moving horse-drawn carts, buses, cabs and other vehicles. The railway was partly in cutting and partly in tunnel, and intermediate stations were situated at Edgware Road, Baker Street, Portland Road (now Great Portland Street), Gower Street (now Euston Square), and Kings Cross. Extension to Moorgate (then Moorgate Street) followed in 1865, Liverpool Street in 1875 and Aldgate in 1876.

This view of Gower Street station (now Euston Square) typifies the earliest design of Metropolitan Railway station. This entirely covered-in design was not satisfactory with conventional steam locomotives and such stations were not repeated until electrification made enclosed surroundings more acceptable.

This engraving of April 1868 shows the Metropolitan & St John's Wood Railway station at Baker Street under construction. In the centre of the picture the sharply curved tunnel leading to the Metropolitan Railway is already complete but the effect of demolition on remaining property is still to be made good.

Subsequent extensions east and west were to produce what are now the Circle and Hammersmith and City Lines, both with trains run by the Met for the majority of their long lives. But the story of today's Metropolitan Line starts not so much with London's first underground line as with London's second, an allied company called the Metropolitan & St John's Wood Railway (MSJWR).

The MSJWR was independently promoted in 1863 and was to run from the Finchley Road area to Baker Street, a distance of 2¼ miles. There were financial links with the Metropolitan, which hoped to gain from the feeder traffic; these went as far as the sharing of offices and some administrative resources. Although parliamentary authorisation came in July 1864 there were serious difficulties in raising money, a recurring theme for London railways. The upshot was that the scope of works was greatly simplified, and the line was constructed single-track from Baker Street to Swiss Cottage only. More money was sought in 1866 as the cost of building even the truncated railway exceeded the expected cost of building the entire enterprise. Although track was not laid any significant distance north of Swiss Cottage, the empty tunnel extended to a point north of the North Star Inn, over a quarter mile through open country immediately beyond the built up area, and was reported to have become something of a playground for local boys.

Agreement was made in 1865 for the line to be worked and staffed by the Metropolitan, necessitating a physical connection between the two systems, authorised in 1867. This took the form of a double junction just east of the Metropolitan station at Baker Street, the signalling for which was controlled from a tiny room built into the angle where the tunnels converged. If nothing else this junction would allow the trains to be serviced by the Metropolitan's facilities at Edgware Road, the new railway not having any of its own. In another event of 1865 the railway obtained powers to extend from Swiss Cottage to Willow Road in Hampstead village, a route involving a ferocious gradient; second thoughts prevailed and this extension was formally abandoned in 1870 with no money raised and no work done.

The MSJWR opened on 13th April 1868 and from a commercial viewpoint could not be regarded as very successful. Neither the main objective at Finchley Road (interchange with the London & North Western Railway) had been achieved, nor had the Hampstead branch, and Swiss Cottage itself was hardly a thriving centre at that time. Admittedly the line ran through the built up area, but it was not densely populated and paralleled a reasonable main road. The limited train services were not, therefore, unduly taxed.

Whilst the line was single track (and almost all in tunnel) the stations at St John's Wood Road, Marlborough Road, and Swiss Cottage were all double track stations in brick-lined cutting, side platforms being provided. Station buildings were single storey brick structures, Marlborough Road surviving to this day as a restaurant.

The MSJWR station at Baker Street, usually referred to as Baker Street East, consisted of two tracks, each with short side platforms from which stairs led up to a building on the north side of Marylebone Road. This was a quite separate facility from the Met station, which then consisted of two subterranean platforms with the street access at their western end (the street buildings, one on each side of Marylebone Road, and the platforms had no physical connection either between themselves or with the East station, so any interchange was awkward).

This Edwardian view of Marlborough Road station gives a good idea of the general arrangement; the building was directly over the railway cutting. The thoroughfare Marlborough Road was renamed Marlborough Place in the 1930s but the station retained the old name until closure.

Through train services initially ran at 20-minute intervals between Swiss Cottage and Moorgate, and during the first summer this was augmented by a local service between Swiss Cottage and Baker Street (East), also at 20-minute intervals and even more poorly patronised. The combined interval of 10-minutes required trains to pass each other at either Marlborough Road or St John's Wood Road, and the 'staff and ticket' system was used with the electric telegraph to prevent two trains meeting on the same single line section (the line could then be operated in three sections). There were conventional signals at each station, but interlocking was rudimentary and there were some minor accidents. From 1874 pilotmen were employed to control the single-line working arrangements instead of the staff and ticket system. This slightly speeded up the overall operation to the point where it was now possible to pass all trains at St John's Wood Road and the number of sections was consequently reduced from three to two – indeed the loop platform at Marlborough Road was taken out of use and the track was removed.

The 'through' trains stopped on 8th March 1869 having proved an operational inconvenience to the Met; two collisions at the start of the year contributed to this view and amongst other things showed that the combined service east of Baker Street was too intense to be operated in a proper manner through the long block sections. From this time a 10-minute 'local' service was maintained on the St John's Wood line. To ease the inconvenience all this caused to the MSJWR's passengers a footbridge was built at the eastern end of the Met's Baker Street platforms, which linked to the East station and provided direct interchange. Thenceforth all 'through' passengers had to change platforms at Baker Street. In due course the double junction connection was singled and the awkward hole-in-the-wall signal box replaced by a more conventional structure built in the junction tunnel in the space vacated – the connection was still necessary for empty stock movements to and from the workshops.

With midday trains running nearly empty, and no prospect of resuming through services to the City, the MSJWR looked to extend to the north-west where it could generate its own new traffic or, by means of a link with another railway, take a share in

A carriage of the 'rigid' 8-wheel variety used on the St John's Wood line from its opening and elsewhere on the Metropolitan system. Just about clear in this photograph are the slightly larger compartments provided for First Class passengers. Also to be noted are the ventilators (only provided for 'smoking' compartments) and the flues for the carriage lamps. LT Museum

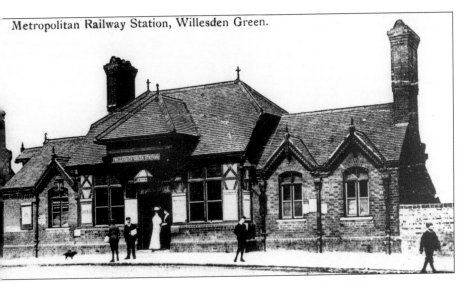

Metropolitan Railway Station, Willesden Green.

This picture postcard of Willesden Green station shows it shortly after opening.
It remained essentially in this form until rebuilt in the 1920s.

theirs. All bets were hedged: the MSJWR Act of 1873 promoted three new lines, all projections north-west of Swiss Cottage. First a railway extending the existing line to the Edgware Road where it would make a connection with the Hampstead Junction Railway, better known now as the North London Line. Next there was a line to the Midland Railway, just west of their Finchley Road station, ready to tap the traffic from the north. Finally there was a third branch of nearly four miles striking out through Willesden to Kingsbury, and terminating in a remote field by the river Brent between Neasdon (using contemporary spelling) and Kingsbury village (long since subsumed by Wembley, the name itself shifting to the north). Access to this then remote site was nevertheless hard won, particularly against the efforts of a certain local landowner, John Prout. He not only won compensation of £180,000 to meet his costs for opposing the railway, but also required it to maintain permanently a station in this vicinity (now Neasden), a rare example of such an obligation placed upon the Underground, and one still in force. By the standard of the time this was a huge price. Nevertheless, the farmland beyond Swiss Cottage in the areas towards and beyond Willesden was beginning to come on to the market for housing development and the MSJWR would have been aware of the need for additional transport facilities into London, potentially filling the empty trains already running. The large tracts of land to be purchased took into account possible future accommodation for workshops which an expanding railway might need at some time in the future. With this major extension in focus, the two smaller extensions were not pursued.

The intended projection to Kingsbury was the last one in which the MSJWR took a wholly independent interest. During the period from 1868 to 1880 the Met had slowly built up its shareholding in the little line and soon gained total practical control. The Metropolitan Railway Act of 1882 required the Met to buy the small remaining shareholding whereupon the MSJWR was to be wound up, a manoeuvre completed with effect from 1st January 1883.

Events to the north

Before considering any further how the Metropolitan Railway expanded out of London, it is necessary to examine how another railway was anxious to move in from the direction of Aylesbury, as this significantly affected events. Matters here were steered by a local enterprise called the Aylesbury & Buckingham Railway (ABR).

The ABR was created by an Act of incorporation of August 1860 with the object of providing a direct line between Claydon and Aylesbury. This was not the first proposal for such a line and reuse of earlier surveys was to make it a near-straight route running to the north of Quainton Hill. The promoters already had the support of Sir Harry Verney, one of the major landowners in the area; the other big landowner was the Marquis of Chandos and in order to engage his support a new route was identified passing Quainton Hill to the south-west and serving more effectively the Marquis's estate at Wotton. In return the Marquis contributed £5000 and volunteered to become chairman – Sir Harry became deputy chairman.

At the northern end the ABR was intended to meet the Bletchley–Oxford line of the London & North Western Railway (LNWR) and at its southern end it was to meet the same railway near their station in Aylesbury, in the prophetically named Dropshort Lane (later Park Street). This station had opened in 1839 at the end of a branch from the main line at Cheddington; the ABR had hopes of running direct trains to London using this route. The ABR took some years to build and was supported only with reluctance by the LNWR (of whose board the Marquis had conveniently also been chairman); one factor was the Marquis's enforced resignation from the board of the LNWR in 1861 when he succeeded to the dukedom of Buckingham & Chandos (he became the third Duke). Without his influence the relationship between the two companies cooled and the LNWR eventually withdrew all support, leaving the ABR in a desperate position as they had neither rolling stock of their own nor money to buy any. However, another possibility arose by virtue of the ABR's relationship with the Great Western Railway (GWR) with whom they intended to share a station in the town.

The Wycombe Railway built a branch to Aylesbury from Princes Risborough which opened on 1st October 1863, the single line being worked by the GWR. By agreement with the ABR, the intention was for both enterprises to own jointly a station at Aylesbury, giving the ABR access to two major railway networks, as well as an option itself to build to the south. The GWR in due course formally absorbed the Wycombe Railway. With the ABR sharing a station with the GWR it was not unnatural in the changed circumstances for them to seek help from that quarter, though there were serious complications; the GWR line was built on the broad gauge and the part-constructed ABR was built on the narrow (now regarded as standard) gauge. However the GWR saw an opportunity to convert their line to standard gauge – which it was contemplating anyway – and obtained a contribution from the ABR of a fifth of the cost. The GWR having saved the day, the incomplete link to the LNWR was abandoned (although it must have been fairly advanced as it is reported that sections of track were discovered in Walton Street, Aylesbury, in the 1950s). The conversion of the GWR

Wycombe branch to standard gauge was accomplished between 14th and 23rd October 1868, and was only the second such gauge conversion on the GWR. The Aylesbury & Buckingham opened without ceremony on 23rd September 1868, which was before the track narrowing in the station had been undertaken, and so requiring temporary platforms to be built just to the north.

The 12¾-mile Aylesbury & Buckingham could hardly be described as a major railway. Beyond Aylesbury the stations on the lightly laid, single-track line were located at Quainton Road, Grandborough Road (Granborough Road from 1920), Winslow Road and Verney Junction. The use of 'Road' suffixes is an ominous reflection on the remoteness of the stations from the villages of those names, while Verney Junction (built by the LNWR at the ABR's cost) was so named by Sir Harry for wont of anything else in the vicinity after which to call it. There were only three trains a day each way, mostly mixed passenger and goods, and these were more than sufficient for the negligible traffic. Inconveniently, through trains over the Wycombe Railway were not run. The line was operated as two single-track sections, with the boundary at Quainton Road. Station staff were all ABR men, though train staff were all GWR. Rolling stock consisted of new 4-wheeled carriages with, of course, provision of first, second and third class accommodation. With GWR operating costs eating up nearly all the revenue the enterprise soon went bankrupt and was put in the hands of a receiver, though it continued to function. The unfortunate ABR had courted the idea of the GWR taking them over, though in the event the matter was allowed to drop.

A great belt of chalk hills stretches across southern Britain diagonally from the south-west to East Anglia, crossing south Buckinghamshire as the Chiltern Hills and forming a serious barrier to railways wishing to approach London from the north. Through some natural gaps in the Chilterns, the main line railways had already monopolised the more important ones. The Wendover gap was still left, through which there were two possible routes to the south, along either the Chess or Misbourne valleys. Whoever built a railway here would have a potentially valuable resource.

This opportunity was not lost on the Duke of Buckingham, who in 1871 was one of the promoters of the grandly named London & Aylesbury Railway. He clearly hoped that by this expedient he could do something to improve the fortunes of the ABR by taking it somewhere more useful. Despite its title the line was intended to run from Aylesbury joint station via the Chess Valley only to Rickmansworth, where it would join the Watford & Rickmansworth Railway by means of an end-on junction (the latter was worked by the LNWR until its absorption by that company in 1881).

It is now necessary to examine the circumstances surrounding the Duke's desire to continue building to the south, and how it happened that the Met planned to meet him by marching north. Even in 1868 an anonymous Metropolitan Railway shareholder was complaining: "It is a mistake that the Metropolitan Railway Company did not confine the line to 4½ miles originally made and opened" and was warning of the dangers of making further expensive extensions likely to impact adversely on dividends (and this followed various irregularities – just exposed – which had evidently been made to disguise poor financial performance). However the Met was already embroiled in further extensions, some very expensive indeed in the City area, and there were to be more serious financial irregularities to the ultimate discredit of the entire board. The outcome was an invitation for a respected railway manager to take charge and Sir Edward Watkin took the chair from 7th August 1872, soon bringing in a new and trusted team. Watkin was also chairman of the Manchester, Sheffield & Lincolnshire and the South Eastern Railways as well as a director of several others.

It was quickly recognised that if suburban traffic were developed it had the advantage of cheaper open-air construction and higher fares which could be charged for the longer journeys, as well as filling up the unused central London capacity. There were already suburban trains on the Met, but these were run by the Great Western, Great Northern, Midland and London Chatham & Dover Railways, all of which were running to Moorgate or Aldgate, though mileage charges due to the Met were not extensive as distances over Metropolitan metals were short. The preponderance of other railways, and the physical geography of north London, made the building of a suburban system difficult to start, but the Met soon identified the Middlesex countryside as a potentially lucrative source of new passengers if and when housebuilding got under way. The existence of the little St John's Wood Railway, connected to the Met, gradually emerged as an obvious solution to the Metropolitan's problems.

With this in mind Watkin was not antagonistic to the MSJWR's desire to build to the north, provided the Met would benefit. It was a matter of concern that the little company was showing a streak of independence that could be damaging in the event that they chose someone else to work the line (or did it themselves) and Watkin seems early on to have set his mind on gaining total control as soon as possible. Assuming he would gain that control (which he soon did) the question was what to do next?

The green fields of Kingsbury never were likely to be entirely satisfactory as a railway terminus. However the only nearby place of any size, and in the same general direction, was Harrow. Though it already had a station on the LNWR, it was hardly a convenient one, being over 1 ½ miles distant from the town. But Harrow was 3 ½ miles from Kingsbury with hardly any intervening population, and neither the Met nor the MSJWR were particularly disposed to rush there. Nevertheless the territory had an obvious interest because of the suburban traffic that could be generated as the areas developed, and there was an immediate opportunity in that the LNWR (whose territory, arguably, it was) did not then seem interested in developing local traffic.

Events were now to move in a new direction. By 1873 Watkin had been colluding with the Duke – still enthusing about railway possibilities to the north of Aylesbury and with authority to get to Rickmansworth in his pocket. The outcome was a proposal for a linking railway built between their respective authorised termini. So it happened that in 1874 two new railway acts emerged: a Kingsbury & Harrow Railway, with Watkin behind it, and a Harrow & Rickmansworth Railway, being pushed by the Duke. Watkin was ambitious, though candid, in his future plans so his exact motives cannot now be known, including whether or not he would have struck north at this time without the Duke's encouragement.

All did not go well. Watkin's energies were much diverted into building the Kingsbury extension over which at first he had merely planned to be an operator. The backing for the London & Aylesbury scheme collapsed and it is perhaps relevant that at the critical moment the Duke accepted an appointment for a 5-year spell as governor of Madras. Without the Aylesbury line there would be no Harrow & Rickmansworth line either. The question was: how would Watkin respond to these events?

Watkin responded by encouraging the Met board to proceed to Harrow anyway, using the Kingsbury & Harrow powers available (though, amidst the uncertainty and with no evidence of any desired housing development, speed was not of the essence). Without the need to join the Harrow & Rickmansworth Railway end-on, the proposed Kingsbury & Harrow station location at Harrow was reconsidered and moved slightly, and then the Met very cautiously started work.

The Kingsbury & Harrow Railway had been authorised in July 1874 and was actually promoted jointly by the Met and the MSJWR; in consequence of the desultory progress the powers had to be extended on several occasions. The authorised railway was to run from Kingsbury (at the proposed terminus of the MSJWR) to Greenhill, at the northern foot of Harrow-on-the-Hill, a distance of roundly 4½ miles. The Act provided for the railway to be worked by a joint committee of the two railways.

While all this was going on it is important to remember that no work whatever had yet been done on the extension from Swiss Cottage to Kingsbury, and the Met decided to build the extensions as one single project. It was not until 1875 that land purchases began in earnest, and construction proper of the extensions did not begin until 1878. The line was to continue from Swiss Cottage in tunnel to a new station on the Finchley Road, thence continue its steady rise from Baker Street through new stations at West Hampstead, Kilburn & Brondesbury, Willesden Green and Kingsbury towards Harrow-on-the-Hill. Near Kilburn the line was to be on a substantial length of viaduct, but otherwise there were to be generally only minor earthworks. Slow progress was made because of harsh weather, and arrangements for opening as far as West Hampstead on 30th June 1879 were temporary – a shuttle train to Swiss Cottage (operating only on the 'down' line), calling at a temporary wooden platform at Finchley Road. However, on 24th November 1879 the full double track railway was available between Swiss Cottage and Willesden Green, with stations largely finished.

Work began beyond Willesden Green early in 1879 and was sufficiently complete for the extension to Harrow-on-the-Hill to open on 2nd August 1880. Kingsbury-Neasden (the proposed Kingsbury terminus, and today's Neasden) was the only intermediate station on this long and very thinly populated section.

The new railway was double-track throughout, but services were initially constrained by the single-track section south of Swiss Cottage. Clearly the original railway now required to be doubled and the work was completed in July 1882, with considerable disruption to the road traffic immediately above. The new tunnel was built on the eastern side of the existing tunnel north of St John's Wood Road, and on the western side to its south.

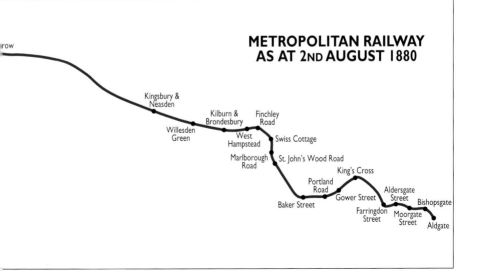

**METROPOLITAN RAILWAY
AS AT 2ND AUGUST 1880**

The trains on the original Swiss Cottage service were drawn from the Met's fleet of 8-wheeled carriages; these were about 40ft long, divided into compartments and were mounted on underframes carried by four axles 'rigidly' fixed in two pairs. The absence of bogies had no effect upon operation on straight track (of which there was comparatively little) but presented serious complications on curves as some lateral movement was essential in at least one axle of each pair if the vehicle was not to derail. Various ingenious methods were resorted to in order for this to be achieved, though in the first batches of carriages it was no more than to allow the axleboxes to slide from side to side within their guides. All trains offered first, second and third class accommodation, either by means of separate carriages or with 'composite' carriages of either first and second, or first and third, compartments. The first class compartments were very well appointed and were deeper than the others (three firsts occupied the same space as four of the others). Variations on these carriages continued to be built until 1884.

From 1869 twenty-six new 4-wheeled carriages predominated on the now isolated St John's Wood line. These were at first arranged in semi-permanently close-coupled pairs whose overall length was about the same as the 8-wheelers. These overcame the complications of curving, but at the expense of a poorer ride quality. This may not have mattered much on the little-used Swiss Cottage service, but when the railway extended to Harrow the 4-wheelers, now travelling at higher speed, did nothing to promote the desired levels of comfort. By 1879 the 4-wheel pairs were modified so that each carriage could operate independently, improving overall flexibility of train formation.

A Harrow train near Harrow around 1900, perhaps with the Sheepcote Road bridge in the background. The train is mainly of 8-wheelers with the third carriage a 4-wheeler. First Class is denoted by white upper panels. Track widening is in progress for the Great Central and the new bridge span is obvious.

At first the Met considered that special locomotives would be needed on the St John's Wood line in order to deal with the difficult gradients – I in 44 either side of the Regents Canal and up to I in 27 on the Hampstead extension. In consequence five powerful 0-6-0 locomotives were especially ordered. However, as the Hampstead extension did not materialise, and as the Met's regular 4-4-0 tank engines were in practice quite comfortable operating the services, the special locomotives were set to one side as expensive to operate. They were eventually sold to the Taff Vale and Sirhowy railways. The 4-4-0s continued to operate the trains when the line was extended to Harrow; the crew in these open-cabbed locomotives were particularly exposed in bad weather and the carriages were all unheated at that time too, neither having been intended for extensive outdoor work.

The stations between Finchley Road and Kingsbury-Neasden were all equipped with side platforms with varying degrees of shelter, each connected to single-storey street-level ticket offices by A. McDermot (although the building at Finchley Road – an area rapidly being built up – was larger and included a refreshment room); today's Neasden station, though somewhat altered, contains some of its original exterior features but the other stations are all now heavily rebuilt.

From the start, signalling on the block system was adopted using entirely mechanically operated signals controlled from signal boxes usually located at each station. The signalman's job was to prevent more than one train being on a section of track at the same time and he was aided in this by the electric telegraph and, from 1882, the gradual introduction of 'lock & block' working where starting signals were locked until positively released by the signalman ahead upon arrival of the previous train.

One feature of the extended line was the provision of a carriage and locomotive works just north of Kingsbury-Neasden station on one of the large tracts of land procured with such a use in sight. By now an efficient workshop facility was an essential ingredient on a rapidly expanding railway and the existing tiny (and increasingly ill-located) facilities at Edgware Road were becoming quite inadequate. The new carriage works (and a gasworks) opened in 1882 and since the whole affair was located in open countryside the railway thoughtfully built over a hundred terraced houses nearby for the staff (much extended in around 1900 and in the early 1920s). The new locomotive works opened in 1883.

Watkin had never intended his trains to go only as far as Harrow, and must have continued to harbour aspirations to make a through route to beyond Aylesbury if he could get there. There is some evidence in the interest he took in Aylesbury connecting railways in the early 1880s, including an extension of the A&B to Towcester, although these ideas may have been sparked off by the Duke, whose interest in promoting railways continued undaunted by practicalities. Nevertheless Watkin had inveigled himself onto the Aylesbury & Buckingham board by 1879 so that he could influence matters more easily.

Without any attempt to hurry things at a time when money was really difficult to raise, Watkin persuaded the Met board to build the Harrow – Aylesbury link itself. New powers were now needed and in 1879 a new bill was deposited (receiving royal assent in August 1880) to create a line extending the Met to Rickmansworth via Pinner and Northwood; the route was similar to the earlier scheme. A further Metropolitan bill, to get the line to Aylesbury, was authorised in July 1881.

Pinner was reached on 25th May 1885, the station there being conveniently situated for the village. The line was opened to Rickmansworth from 1st September

1887 (after some contractual difficulties) and an hourly service was provided. The only intermediate station was Northwood. Rickmansworth station itself followed the general pattern except in that it was built on a sharp curve owing to successful objections from landowners to a more straightforward route, thus creating permanent inconvenience for passengers and a heavy speed restriction which was particularly unfavourable to northbound trains faced with an immediate and steep uphill grade.

Work began on the Aylesbury extension in 1886. However, the route adopted took the line along the Misbourne valley, which missed Chesham. As this town was of some substance the Act had provided for it to be served by means of a branch line, as a station on the main line would have been too far away. The branch resulted from considerable local pressure – supported by a locally raised contribution of £2000 so a conveniently located station could be built – and an observation by the Met that it would make a suitable springboard from which Tring might be reached (such a line was authorised in the Metropolitan Railway Act 1885, but not proceeded with; at that time there was barely the money to get to Aylesbury).

The Met had even more difficulty raising money than previously. Attempts to get landowners to support construction against an issue of shares was predictably unsuccessful and shows the state of desperation into which the railway had fallen. In consequence it was decided in the first instance to extend the line from Rickmansworth to Chesham only, and this was opened on 8th July 1889; it was double track via Chorleywood as far as the other intermediate station at Chalfont Road, and single track beyond. The main line between Chalfont Road and Aylesbury eventually opened on 1st September 1892, with intermediate stations at Amersham, Great Missenden, Wendover and Stoke Mandeville.

A London bound train arriving at Great Missenden before the First World War. The station is typical of those on the Aylesbury line and the distinctive canopies are a feature still evident today. The station hasn't changed very much since opening but is somewhat busier today than the photo suggests it might have been in times gone by.

THE RAILWAY STATION, GT. MISSENDEN.

The are few photographs of the Aylesbury & Buckingham Railway prior to Metropolitan operation. This view (looking south) shows the joint Great Western and Aylesbury & Buckingham station at Aylesbury. It seems the GWR had priority to use the platform with the buildings. The wide track spacing is a relic of broad gauge operation.

The question must now be posed about what Watkin proposed to do having reached Aylesbury, some 38 miles from Baker Street. For most of the schemes to the north in which he had shown interest it seemed that a vital component was the absorption of the tiny but critically-located Aylesbury & Buckingham, which was already under Watkin's influence. Investment was needed, together with more direct control. Consequently, purchase by the Met took place on 1st July 1891 for £150,000 (it had cost £167,000 to build). Unfortunately the line was so lightly constructed that the Met found it had no suitable locomotives that could operate and had temporarily to rely on the LNWR to run the service. However, with optimism undaunted the Met set about repairing, upgrading and doubling the line, an activity completed in 1894. The rebuilt ABR comprised a double line of railway throughout. Each station was rebuilt with two platforms with Quainton Road resited further south. At Verney Junction the Met used the southern face of the island platform otherwise used for Oxford trains, and the junction with the Bletchley–Oxford line was at the western end; with the rebuilding, extensive sidings were built at the London end for the exchange of goods traffic. A new station, called Waddesden Manor, was built between Quainton Road and Aylesbury and opened on 1st January 1897. The opportunity was also taken to replace 12 level crossings with bridges, leaving just two remaining.

Aylesbury station, though always two-track, had at first only been equipped with a platform on the 'up' side, a second platform not appearing until the gauge narrowing had been undertaken; nevertheless for many years most trains of both the ABR and GWR continued to use the up platform as it was more convenient.

The arrival of the Met in 1892 gave rise to the need to remodel Aylesbury station. As the work was not ready in time a temporary terminus was opened, known as Brook Street, a little to the south; this comprised a single wooden platform on the 'up' line reached by a temporary facing crossover. Locos ran forward into the yard prior to running round the train via the down line. This station went out of use on 1st January 1894 when Met trains were extended into the joint station, requiring them to negotiate a very sharp double junction later to be the subject of complaints about unsafe speeding that culminated in a serious accident and relaying on a straighter alignment. For a while local trains continued to provide the Verney Junction–Aylesbury service, but through services to London began operating from 1st January 1897. Meanwhile, Aylesbury station had been remodelled with the previously little-used 'down' platform being replaced by a new island, having facilities for the terminating GWR trains to use the western face; this time a passenger shelter and footbridge were provided. The buildings on the up platform were little altered. A bay road was later provided alongside the northern platform, mainly for the use of the Met.

At this point the existence of another line needs to be mentioned. It was noted earlier that the Aylesbury & Buckingham had been diverted to run nearer to the Duke's estate near Waddesdon. It is recorded that the Duke had it in mind to operate his own private tramway to service his land, and that he wanted it linked somewhere with a main line railway. Work began in September 1870 using his own labourers who had less other work to do during the winter months. The first section came into use on 1st April 1871 between Quainton Road station and Kingswood via Wotton Underwood, the Duke organising a small ceremony to mark the occasion. Later during the year it extended in stages from Wotton to Thame Lodge, Wood Siding and Brill brickworks, leaving the Kingswood section as a branch. In March the following year it reached its final terminus at the foot of Brill Hill, and ¾-mile from the town at the top of that hill.

The line was originally very lightly laid and intended purely for moving goods and materials around the estate. Estate workers were carried and, seeing this, the local community declared a desire to use the line, which began to carry passengers at the beginning of 1872 – rather unusual for a non-statutory railway. The early passenger service operated no more than twice daily and used an ancient borrowed 4-wheeled carriage which at first took over 90 minutes (later reduced to 70) to complete the 6¼-mile journey. Stations – or boarding points might be a better term – were at Quainton Road, Waddesdon Road, Westcott, Wotton (on the Ashendon–Dorton road), Church Siding (near Wotton Underwood at the junction with the Kingswood branch), Wood Siding and Brill. The section from Wotton to Kingswood (often known as Church Siding) was about a mile, but it was only ever worked by horses and never (officially) carried passengers; it was closed around 1910 and the rails soon lifted except for a short spur running as far as Wotton Underwood village. The terminus at Kingswood (the hamlet was nearly a mile away) was next to the road running to the north of Wotton Park, and lay in very remote country. Horse power was the only form of traction at opening and the track was laid with longitudinal timbers such that horses could proceed with ease; these arrangements were quickly proved wanting and in 1872 a pair of tramway locomotives were obtained but these machines had a top speed of only 8 mph and were just modified traction engines.

This quite unimportant private tramway would in all probability have faded gradually out of existence had it not been for another railway scheme promoted by Sir Harry Verney and the Duke of Buckingham (fresh back from India). This time additional support was lent by Baron Ferdinand de Rothschild, who lived at Waddesdon. The improbably named Oxford, Aylesbury and Metropolitan Junction Railway, created in November 1882, was intended to be a 17½-mile line linking Quainton Road and Oxford, single-track at first, but with provision for doubling (it would then have been the shortest route from the City of London to Oxford, but only by 2 miles). The Duke had considered such a scheme as part of his 1873 contemplations and was strongly attracted to the need to link Oxford with Aylesbury.

As the new railway was to be built to normal railway standards the private Brill tramway was by and large unsuitable for incorporation, but there were many places between Quainton and Brill where the tramway was in the way and a few where its alignment was useful for a little way. However the enabling Act passed the following year sought to preserve the integrity of the tramway in the event that the Duke did not require his new venture to purchase it. Unable to raise the capital for this expensive scheme, a new and simpler one was put forward which received the royal assent in August 1888. Called the Oxford and Aylesbury Tramroad, it provided for a significant upgrading of the existing tramway (which it would purchase or rent), plus an extension to Oxford along a less expensive route. After many serious tribulations and setbacks (including the death both of the Duke and Sir Harry), the tramway was leased from the estate by the O&AT on 1st April 1894. It had been intended to purchase the freehold, but there was never the money to do so.

While the penniless O&AT never got beyond Brill, the existing tramway was rebuilt on slightly more conventional lines and with minor realignment; as primitive stations developed from the timing points, Church Siding 'station' disappeared as it was very close to Wotton. The successor to most of the estate, Earl Temple of Stowe, was content for all links with the estate to be severed at a formal level so that in most respects the line became a normal, if very minor and idiosyncratic, railway concern. Even the ponderous tram engines were eventually replaced by small 0-6-0 locomotives, though far from new, and the railway joined the Railway Clearing House so that through traffic could be booked. The Board of Trade inspected the line and made various comments including an observation that the O&AT should obtain parliamentary sanction for the various level crossings on the line in its next bill; in the event this was never done as the railway never needed to go back to parliament for anything else. In 1899 the train service had improved to four a day each way (of mixed goods and passenger formation) and the journey time had dropped to a mere 40 minutes for the fastest train.

The arrival of the Metropolitan Railway at Quainton Road offered the opportunity for something to be done with the moribund O&AT, who saw no possibility of ever reaching Oxford. Discussions with the Met took place with a view to possible takeover, pending which the latter agreed to work the line pro tem, an offer made in November 1899 and taken up by the O&AT. The Met never did buy the line but by virtue of that offer letter they did begin to work it, slowly resulting in further improvements to the track and the construction of short, standard height platforms made out of sleepers and earth. Reaching over 50 miles from London, this rural backwater was now on the 'Underground'.

More frequent train services brought about by the extensions required some improvements at Baker Street (East). The original 2-platform layout was thus superseded by one with four platform faces, though in unusual formation. The track leading into the single-track link with the Circle Line received a platform face on each side, with the eastern platform being an island serving a bay road. Next to it was a further bay road with another platform beyond that. The two bay roads converged on a 'sector plate' (a kind of turntable which could be used to switch locomotives from one bay into the other – this was problematical and it was later removed and an 'escape' crossover installed instead so that locomotives could be released). Usually a drawbridge covered the infrequently used single-track connection allowing a level route for passengers changing platforms.

During this period of expansion there was only marginal development of the railway's services within Middlesex. The only new local station to be built before the turn of the century was Wembley Park, and this was hardly because of pressing local demand – quite the opposite. Perceiving a need to find ways of generating new traffic, the Met had in 1890 purchased a large area of land on the south side of the line between Kingsbury-Neasden and Harrow, and known as Wembley Park. It was proposed to develop part of the area for housing and part as a sports, leisure and exhibition centre crowned by a massive tower (of 1150ft) inspired by the success of Eiffel's tower in Paris, completed in 1889 at a mere 984ft. It was hoped such an attraction would generate much new traffic from London.

Wembley Park station was first opened on 14th October 1893 for the use of the 'Old Westminster's Football Club' (and again on 21st) but regular opening was postponed until the park itself was opened to the public on 12th May 1894. Platforms were at first built alongside the up and down lines but, doubtless to deal with the throngs of people who were to teem in from London, additional facilities were decided upon. These included a pair of platforms on the north side (leading into sidings at the 'country' end), one served by the other face of the up platform and the most northerly one having a platform of its own; the additional platforms were ready for the 1894 opening. None of the platforms were at first covered in any way, and from each steps led up to a station building on the road bridge at the eastern end. But the people didn't come, and the terminal facilities were largely devoted to the storage of dead trains. Although the first 155ft high stage of the tower was completed (only a fifth of the final height) difficult money and general lack of interest meant the abandonment of the scheme, though the much later emergence of Wembley stadium on the very same site meant that some of the original aspirations were to be met.

To facilitate construction of the station a pair of sidings was built on the 'down' side of the line just north of the platforms. These also proved useful in providing facilities for construction of the tower to which a temporary railway was laid down. Leaving the sidings facing west the line curved south on a short embankment to cross Brook Avenue and the Wealdstone Brook. It then ran along the west side of Raglan Gardens (now Empire Way) for about 300 yards at a rising gradient of 1:31 before turning west, rising at 1:25 and terminating at the foot of the tower. The line was standard gauge and used some of the rails recently recovered from the Aylesbury & Buckingham railway; four 40ft timbers were used to get the line across the Wealdstone Brook, and it was complete by the end of January 1893. The Met is believed to have provided one of its own locomotives to supply motive power. With the abandonment of construction works the tower line became derelict for a while, but was re-invigorated prior to its lifting by the need to help with the demolition works in 1904.

By the turn of the century service patterns had settled down. Outside the peak

Wembley Park station in 1902, with horse and carriage awaiting custom. The stations further north were generally somewhat larger and situated in their own platform level approach road, usually on the London-bound side.

hours there was a basic 10-minute service between Willesden Green and Baker Street calling at all stations. During each hour, four of these trains started at Willesden Green, one came all-stations from Harrow, and one all-stations from Rickmansworth. Trains from Verney Junction ran only two-hourly calling all stations to Harrow, thence Willesden Green (connecting into local services), and non-stop to Baker Street. Of course, these long distance trains shared the same tracks as the local services and it was fortunate that, in leaving Willesden Green immediately prior to a local service, the scheduling allowed the non-stop run without quite catching up the previous all-stations train – at least in theory. During the peaks trains were a little more frequent, the locals mainly starting from Kingsbury-Neasden, the Rickmansworth trains (some coming through from Chesham) running non-stop south of Willesden, and the Verney Junction trains running non-stop from Harrow. One or two trains originated at West Hampstead or Kilburn. On Sundays the off peak pattern was followed except south of Willesden, where the pattern was based on a 15-minute rather than 10-minute cycle. From Chesham, apart from the few through trains, the remaining service was provided by a shuttle train terminating at Chalfont Road in a bay road at the back of the 'up' platform.

All this expansion brought forward a need for additional locomotives and rolling stock. The original Beyer-Peacock 4-4-0T design proved robust and additional broadly similar locos were purchased until 1885, by which time there were 66 in operation; they were capable of obtaining some speed on the Aylesbury line, 60 mph or more being recorded. They were rebuilt at various times but retained their general overall appearance although some were fitted with cabs. In 1891 four 0-4-4T locomotives similar to a South Eastern railway design were obtained from Neilson's, followed by six 2-4-0Ts from Sharp Stewart in 1894/5. The Met itself designed the next batch, an 0-4-4T design, of which it built two at Neasden in 1896, and a further one in 1898 to replace an earlier loco damaged in an accident. Four more were ordered from Hawthorn Leslie and entered service in 1900/1. The final batch built prior to electrification was of four 0-6-2Ts of the F class built by the Yorkshire Engine Company which entered service in 1901. By this time the fleet was of 91 locomotives (including the Oxford & Aylesbury machines); all were tank engines avoiding the need for constant turning at each end of the journey. The total also included three smaller tanks built (in 1886, 1897 and 1899) for shunting use at Neasden and the larger goods yards.

From 1887 the original 4-wheeled carriages were supplemented by a new 4-wheeled design built by Cravens and arranged to run in three trains of nine close-coupled vehicles each, of which two were first class, two second class and five third; these became known as the Jubilee stock, inspired by the royal event of that year. The first-class carriages had four compartments while the others had five each. A further four trains were purchased in 1892 for the extension to Aylesbury, this time of 8-vehicle formation designed to be split (if necessary) at Chalfont Road to provide a Chesham portion (but this arrangement was abandoned in 1896 and the trains were converted to permanent full length sets).

Short 4-wheeled carriages were really not very satisfactory on the long runs out to Aylesbury and between 1898 and 1900, 54 vehicles of 'bogie' stock were constructed. The first four 6-carriage close-coupled trains were built by the Ashbury Railway Carriage & Iron Company, with subsequent batches ordered from Ashbury's (two further sets), Cravens of Sheffield (two sets), and one set constructed by the Met itself at Neasden. These carriages were each around 40ft long. Carriages had seven second or third-class compartments but the firsts and composite firsts had only six compartments each.

The earliest Met carriages used gas lighting, coal gas being carried in large, weighted bags mounted in the roof and occasionally recharged from suitable points along the line from the metered gas mains. This was viewed as a considerable improvement over the oil lamps used by other railways, even if the gas had to be recharged every three hours. The Jubilee stock was equipped from the outset with the 'Pintsch' lighting system, which involved carrying compressed oil gas that did not need recharging as frequently, and in due course older carriages were modified. Amongst other places, an oil gas production plant was installed at Baker Street but it was not popular with the railway's neighbours because of the smell produced and the Met was forced to consolidate this operation at Neasden, where neighbours were few and mainly on the staff. Compressed gas was then conveyed to storage vessels around the network by special gas holder vehicles, as carriages which didn't stable overnight at Neasden needed to be recharged. The bogie stock was equipped with electric light from the outset, operating on the 'Stones' system that relied on batteries when a train was stationary and an axle-driven dynamo when it was moving. Open-air running also created a need for heating, not provided on the first carriages at all, or on the Jubilee stock at first though they were later equipped with steam heating coils. The bogie stock had heating from the outset.

Another important feature on a railway operating at frequent intervals at least partly in dark, smoke-filled tunnels is the ability for its trains to be able to stop fairly promptly. Originally braking was provided on the locomotive and from handbrakes at the front and rear of each train controlled by front and rear guards, all operated quite independently of each other. This manifestly unsatisfactory form of operation was soon superseded by Wilkins and Clark's chain brake involving a cord carried across the

One of the Metropolitan's fleet of 4-wheeled coaches used throughout its network. They would not have been immensely comfortable to travel in. LT Museum

This pre-First World War view of Great Missenden shows a station exterior typical of those on the Aylesbury extension. Station buildings were usually on the London-bound side. The areas served by the Aylesbury extension became popular but were not densely built up, so the use of a car was handy though for many years a luxury. The car in this photo (registered in Bristol) would appear to be driven by a chauffeur. C. Seabright

carriage roofs which, by means of weights and pulleys, allowed the engine drivers to apply what had been the carriage handbrakes from the locomotive. This had some very significant drawbacks but was judged an improvement over what had previously prevailed. From 1875 Smith's simple vacuum brake was adopted (a vast improvement) and this was soon converted into a fully automatic brake, which at last produced an effective and fail-safe braking mechanism broadly compatible with most other railways. Nevertheless a passenger operated emergency brake was not provided on the steam stock despite encouragement made by the Railway Inspectorate (it was not then mandatory for short distance trains) and notwithstanding an attempted murder in 1910 between Baker Street and Swiss Cottage. Passenger alarms were delivered on some vehicles from new but were not universal until 1932.

While the Met was finishing its extension to Aylesbury, Watkin became ill and resigned the chairmanship of the Met and his other companies in May 1894. Without his machinations there was little prospect of any further interest by the Met in expanding beyond Verney Junction, a forever-remote location that, with hindsight, the Met would rather not have visited in the first place. However, Watkin had left behind him something which would very shortly put all this effort on to the English main line railway map, and this now needs to be examined.

Sir Edward Watkin's preoccupation with making the Met connect into a main line railway, about which the Met board itself seems to have been ambivalent, finally came to fruition when he persuaded his Manchester, Sheffield & Lincolnshire Railway to invest in a highly expensive and ultimately irrelevant 99-mile orgy of construction from its established territory in south Yorkshire to London, meeting the Met just north of Quainton Road. Quite what Watkin's ultimate motives were are now unknown, though even as long previously as 1860 he had indicated an aspiration for the MS&LR to get independent access to London (it did run some London trains using running powers over other railways). By the end of 1871 he had revealed that he was contemplating using the Metropolitan Railway as a part of this link, not wholly unreasonable given that the emerging Met then seemed likely to have the spare capacity and was not in a competitive position. It is often claimed Watkin had a grand scheme to use his railways as a through route from Manchester to a Channel tunnel (another scheme he had an interest in) but there is little real evidence for this.

At first he had designs on Baker Street as the trunk line's terminus. This might have been to facilitate the operation of cross-London trains but more probably it was no more complicated than avoidance of heavy cost of purchasing land in central London. However, during 1891–2 the MS&LR had concluded that it needed its own facilities in the Marylebone area, mainly to accommodate the very substantial goods yard (which was really the point of the extension) and this facilitated the building of a 'proper' terminus (with adjacent hotel) at the same time. It is difficult now to understand how even the most optimistic railway manager could seriously have considered that the cramped Baker Street site would ever have sufficed, though the Met was most anxious to promote it and would have gained considerable revenue had things happened that way. Even with a separate terminus the link to the Met was not forgotten, and was to be by means of a tunnel under the hotel intended to join the Circle Line half way between Edgware Road and Baker Street. All this was provided for in the MS&LR's authorising bill, passed after some delays, in March 1893.

Watkin's resignation effectively separated MS&LR and Met interests completely, and for a while the relationship between them became quite sour. Even though work on the extension began in October 1894, all was no longer well. The MS&LR powers had allowed for the Marylebone line to begin at Canfield Place, just north-west of Finchley Road station, but the Met would be widened on the north side until a point just north of West Hampstead, facilitating goods interchange with other railways in the area. Disagreement blew up with the Met about the arrangements for this, fuelled further by concerns over the usage of the tracks north of West Hampstead. A Metropolitan Railway report of 1895 demonstrated that this had suddenly become a matter of great concern. The conclusion was that with the existing service of 19 trains in the busy 2-hour morning period at West Hampstead, it was in theory possible to slot in ten of the new company's trains, implying an offering of five trains an hour throughout the day (with more at night), a maximum daily offering of 250 trains. This was thought reasonable – at least by the Met – by comparison with the service on similar railways into London. Only moderate additional infrastructure was contemplated, in particular another signal box would be needed near Villiers Road, between Kingsbury-Neasden and Wembley Park, to reduce the headways on that section. The Manchester company, on the other hand, were not content with this and indignantly pointed out that use of huge numbers of theoretical 'slots' during the night was not at all what they had in mind and they wanted daytime capacity which would inevitably clash with the Met's services south of Kingsbury-Neasden.

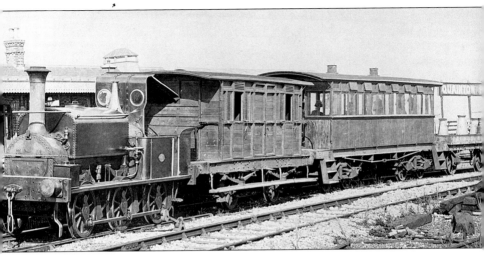

Brill tramway train with *Huddersfield* at **Quainton Road** in 1900. LT Museum

The outcome was the Met agreeing to construct a second pair of tracks between Wembley Park and Canfield Place, parallel to the first pair and intended for the exclusive use of the MS&LR. This required some significant earthworks without disturbing the existing railway. The new line was built entirely to the south of the older lines. It was consistently believed that the existing Metropolitan Railway between Quainton Road and Wembley Park could easily accommodate the trains of the new railway, renamed the Great Central Railway (GCR) in 1897; with existing Met services of only two or three trains an hour, this was perhaps not unreasonable. In the event, the need to improve structures north of Wembley Park to suit the GCR's rolling stock resulted in the Met extending the four-track scheme all the way to Harrow. GCR passenger trains first served the new Marylebone terminus from March 1899, initially using existing Met tracks for most of the way north of Canfield Place; some temporary connections were made to the Met whilst the new works were being built, but the new lines finally came into exclusive GCR use in March 1901.

Construction challenges on the newly widened lines had an impact on the Met's existing facilities. At West Hampstead there was insufficient space for the new tracks and the Met 'down' platform had to be removed; the existing 'up' platform was thus converted into an island (the first at an intermediate station on the Met) and the tracks re-arranged to suit. A pair of sidings was installed just north of the station at the same time, and the opportunity was taken to construct a larger station building. In 1906 the Met and GCR entered into a new agreement, and as part of this the new tracks between Harrow and Canfield Place were leased to the GCR for 999 years, though the Met retained the freehold.

The Metropolitan District Railway, an errant and now highly independent child of the Met, had managed to invade Met territory with its Ealing & South Harrow Railway (E&SHR) which had been authorised in 1894 and whose construction was in progress at the turn of the century. The line began at a junction with the District near Ealing Common and meandered gently towards the village of Roxeth, nearly the same distance south of Harrow-on-the-Hill as the Met was to its north.

But the District's aspirations went beyond even South Harrow. The market town of Uxbridge had interest to the District as a traffic objective, if not beyond. Some activity was spawned in 1891–2 when a route was surveyed, but no bill was then deposited. In 1896 the District felt able to take some action and a bill was deposited for a nominally independent line making an end-on junction with the E&SHR at South Harrow and proceeding to High Wycombe, via Ruislip and Uxbridge (where it would link with an Uxbridge & Rickmansworth scheme). Great Western opposition saw off the Wycombe section but the line from South Harrow to Uxbridge was authorised in 1897, creating the Harrow & Uxbridge Railway. This was to be worked by the District which would retain receipts and pay interest on the capital costs; the act also made provision for eventual take over by the District.

As was often the case, fund-raising proved difficult and this was not helped by much of the route being very thinly populated. The Metropolitan Railway offered to rescue the scheme (having had eyes on Uxbridge itself when promoting an unsuccessful Act in 1881) and an Act of 1899 was passed which authorised a link from Harrow-on-the-Hill to a junction with the Harrow & Uxbridge where it was crossed by Rayners Lane, then a remote trackway. The District retained limited running powers for up to three trains per hour between South Harrow and Uxbridge. Construction work started in 1901 and took about three years. Met trains to Uxbridge began on 4th July 1904; the only intermediate station along the line (described as 'mainly grassland') was at Ruislip, commodious facilities being built there for passengers and goods. For the time being the Met-owned link to South Harrow remained out of use, in apparent contravention of the terms of the 1899 Act which required the whole of the original Harrow & Uxbridge to be opened for traffic before the Harrow–Rayners Lane section was opened.

Meanwhile, the character of the main line north of Harrow was about to change owing to the arrival of the Great Central Railway, risking a conflict of interest between the attention given to GCR main line passenger and freight services on the one hand and local Met services on the other (at a time when there were other tensions between the railways). Two real issues arose. First there was ongoing suspicion by the GCR about the Met's ability to handle both types of traffic satisfactorily despite the new tracks. Secondly the GCR had easy curves and gradients (permitting comparatively high speed) while the Met section had severe gradients and some very sharp curves. Consequently, as early as 1897, the GCR was seeking to conclude an agreement with the Great Western for an alternative route into London via Aynho and Beaconsfield. The GWR proved co-operative and it was

soon agreed to construct a new line jointly with the Great Western that would allow GCR trains to divert from their existing line just north of Quainton Road and rejoin it at Neasden, avoiding the Met tracks completely. This left the Met very unhappy at the prospect of losing very valuable GCR revenue (and abortive Met expenditure) but they were able to extract an agreement for a degree of compensation.

When the dust had settled and the relationship between the companies had improved it was decided to place control of those of the Met's lines used by the GCR into the hands of a separate management body that would represent both interests. As part of this the following agreement was reached.

The new tracks between Harrow South Junction and Canfield Place would be leased to the GCR for 999 years at an annual rental of £20,000 a year, with Met retaining running powers on the northern section, and a flat crossing at Wembley Park so the Met could retain access to its goods yard which was on the south-west side of the line. The Met would lease its railway between Harrow South Junction and Verney Junction (including Chesham but excluding the Uxbridge branch) to a statutory joint committee (the Metropolitan & Great Central Joint Committee) for 999 years at a rent of £44,000 annually. The Met's interest in the Brill tramway would be passed to the Joint Committee. The GCR would put a minimum of £45,000 a year's worth of traffic on to the line. The day-to-day management of the Committee's operations would rest for alternate 5-year periods with each party, beginning with the Met.

The new arrangements came into force on 2nd April 1906. All these gave the Met a degree of assured traffic and addressed the compensation issue that had been hanging around for nearly ten years. The management of Aylesbury station deserves a mention. It had at first been run jointly by the Great Western and the Met (as successors to the Aylesbury & Buckingham). However, the former Wycombe line had been handed over to the control of the Great Western & Great Central Joint Committee, while the Met's interest had now passed to the Metropolitan & Great Central Joint Committee. The outcome was that Aylesbury joint station found itself in the hands of a joint committee of the two joint committees, producing an unworkably long title the use of which was circumvented where possible by use of the name Aylesbury Joint Station.

The operation of the Met&GC Joint Committee can conveniently be divided into three: day-to-day operations, management and accounting. The first of these was in the hands of the local station staff that became employees of the Joint Committee itself (the term station staff also included goods staff and signalmen, etc; train services were always supplied separately by both the Met and the Great Central railways and their successors as the Joint Committee had no rolling stock of its own, except a crane). Management and accounting were intended to be supplied in alternating periods of five years by both the owning companies, with the Met doing the 'management' for the first five years with the Great Central doing the 'accounting', then switching over, and so on. Found to be wasteful, the arrangements were later changed, and from 1926 'management' stayed with the Met. Even at the beginning it was recognised that certain activities were not amenable to constant changing, and track maintenance was one of them. With some logic the Met assumed control of maintenance from milepost 28½ (south of Great Missenden) and the Great Central to the north, which roughly equalised mileage. The operation of the goods services was particularly wasteful as for a while each provided motive power in turns of only a fortnight; this was addressed from 1910 when the Met provided all motive power at favourable rates. In the case of Aylesbury Joint Station, a similar system of rotating responsibilities was adopted, this time including the Great Western, and this continued until the Second World War.

Electrification

As the twentieth century dawned, falling traffic fuelled by competition from buses, trams and the new all-electric 'tube' railways, badly worried both the Met and the District railways. It was realised that the grimy, smoke filled carriages and gloomy and congested sub surface stations which characterised the central London sections were now quite unacceptable. The only way forward was complete modernisation based on electrical operation. Various options presented themselves.

To test one of the proposed electrical systems, well-publicised experiments were conducted jointly with the District Railway in 1900 between Earl's Court and High Street Kensington using a dc system using two conductor rails. However, the Met was interested in conducting its own experiments, and the moribund Wembley 'tower' railway was examined for its possible use, a matter agreed to in April 1899. Twin conductor rails of steel channel were laid. Two carriages (similar to the bogie stock) were built at Neasden works and these were intended to be equipped with four motors each and a form of series-parallel electrical control. Contractual difficulties surrounded the supply of generating equipment, but makeshift arrangements were put in place involving a withdrawn 4-4-0 locomotive jacked up and connected mechanically to a pair of dynamos by a drive belt (actually the dynamos were a pair of the motors adapted for the purpose). The experiments are believed to have lasted about a year and were evidently satisfactory. The carriages lay idle for a while but eventually entered revenue-earning service with one surviving until 1962.

A driving motor car of 1904 stock provided for the Metropolitan electrification scheme. This particular view shows the end gangway having been enclosed and centre doors fitted (all these doors were sliding and hand operated by passengers).

Although a low voltage direct current system using twin conductor rails worked satisfactorily at both Earl's Court and Wembley, the Met and the District were briefly persuaded of the benefits of a high tension alternating current system developed by Ganz in Budapest. This was a 3000 Volt 3-phase system that required twin overhead wires. The overall economics of the operation looked very attractive. For example only a quarter of the substations would have been needed, the energy losses would have been much lower and regeneration was possible. However, it was then untried and caution won the day with the low voltage dc system eventually being selected. The Ganz system, incidentally, was soon in operation on the Lake Como railway and was very successful with the result that 3-phase ac railways spread quite widely on the continent. Its particular suitability and economy for comparatively long distance operation would almost certainly have resulted in the entire Met system having been converted sooner rather than later, but it was not to be.

After looking at a site at Edgware Road the Met decided to build its own power station on land just north of Neasden works; this meant electrification from Baker Street to at least Neasden was called for, as well as its in-town railway comprising the northern part of the Circle Line. At the time the Uxbridge branch was still under construction and it also seemed sensible to build it as an electrified railway (the 1899 Act had especially provided for electric as well as steam operation).

Neasden generating station was convenient for coal to be delivered by rail and for water to be obtained from two (three from 1919) deep artesian wells. The main building was 101ft wide and 325ft long (extended later to 481ft). The plant was supplied by the British Westinghouse Electric and Manufacturing Company and comprised three (soon four) 3.5MW generators driven by Westinghouse turbines running at 1000 rpm. The generators supplied 3-phase current at 11kV and 33⅓ cycles per second; they could operate at 50 per cent overload for up to an hour which was a useful feature during extreme peak loading. Steam was raised by means of 14 Babcock & Wilcox boilers. The water was cooled in cooling towers and a lake. Coal was brought by rail direct to the station and then taken by conveyors to the various coal hoppers over the boilers.

Power was conveyed at high tension to substations at Baker Street, Finchley Road, Neasden, Harrow-on-the-Hill and Ruislip, at each of which transformers and multiple 800kW rotary converters (1200kW at Baker Street) reduced the voltage to around 600V dc. At this voltage it was fed to a pair of conductor rails, one centred between the running rails and the other just outside on one side. The above substations comprised generally three converters, though there were four at Neasden and only two at Ruislip. Additional substations were provided on the Met's Inner Circle section.

The Met (or perhaps, more accurately, its contractor British Westinghouse) was unlucky with the equipment of this power station; spectacularly sooty and gritty smoke soon required it to completely replace the coal feeding equipment and following a number of unfortunate serious failures the generators soon required rewinding (the Underground Group's power station at Lots Road also suffered from these sorts of difficulty). The long drawn out financial settlement of the claims against the manufacturer included modification of the turbines and rewinding the four generators for 5MW. A fifth 5MW turbo-generator was installed in 1908 together with six additional boilers, making a total of twenty.

The first electric multiple unit train entered regular passenger service on the Baker Street to Uxbridge all-stations service on 1st January 1905, and by the end of March 1905 the all-stations trains between Baker Street and Harrow (and Uxbridge) were all electric. The very poorly patronised Uxbridge through trains to and from London were quickly replaced by shuttles between Uxbridge and Harrow. The District Railway began exercising its running powers between South Harrow and Uxbridge in 1910, whereupon the Met shuttles were reduced further, from three vehicles to single-vehicle trains, special carriages with a cab at each end being then available. The service on the Uxbridge branch became so thin that it was found possible to mothball Ruislip (later called Ickenham) substation and for some years the entire branch was fed from Harrow.

Initially the trains north of Baker Street comprised new saloon coaches intended for service mainly on the Inner Circle; quite arbitrarily saloon vehicles came to be referred to as 'coaches' rather than 'carriages'. The initial batches consisted of motor coaches (with a driving cab at one end) and trailers, each about 52ft 6ins long. Entrances were provided only at the car ends by means of open platforms that were not really suitable for extensive open-air working. Accommodation was provided for first and third class passengers (second class was abolished on Met trains north of Baker Street from 1st February 1905). Third class coaches had buffalo hide seats in both transverse and longitudinal arrangement while first class accommodation had more elaborate interiors with green leather seats in the smoking sections and 'art green' moquette in non-smoking sections. Bevelled mirrors and photographs of interesting places in areas served by the Met completed the scene.

Much of the older steam-hauled stock was either disposed of or laid up, but the comparatively new bogie carriages now existed in larger numbers than were required for the infrequent steam trains on the Aylesbury line and were felt worth converting to electric operation. An early idea was to haul 4-carriage bogie trains as far as Harrow with one of the new electric motor coaches and thence by steam locomotive; two trains were made available but in the event they were little used for this purpose. From 1905, the better (but more expensive) solution was adopted of converting the 3rd class brake carriages into electric motor vehicles by installing glazing and driving apparatus in the brake compartments and fitting the necessary electrical gear. An appropriate number of the other carriages were equipped with through control lines and the Westinghouse air brake instead of the vacuum brake. Some seven 6-coach trains were so converted and these operated the longer journeys where possible; the saloon stock trains were relegated to use on the shorter journeys only. Later batches of saloon cars were introduced to meet demand elsewhere and these had enclosed end platforms from the start; the earlier cars soon had these platforms enclosed. The end doors (and subsequently the new doors in the centre too) were sliding but hand operated. Train formations generally stabilised at six coaches, which proved the maximum convenient for the shorter platforms; the first-class trailers (which were generally in the middle of the train) all became driving trailers, allowing short trains of three coaches to be run as necessary. Nevertheless, until housing development took off between the wars these saloon coaches tended to operate only in the central area.

The loco-hauled trains from Pinner and beyond continued to be steam-operated for a while, though some steam trains were reversed at Wembley Park where passengers were expected to change for an electric train to Baker Street. Matters improved when electric locomotives became available, and from 1st January 1907 all trains south of Wembley Park were electrically hauled, with steam and electric locomotives being switched there. The locomotive change-over point more logically became Harrow in 1908 when station alterations were complete.

The first batch of electric locomotives consisted of ten machines ordered from

A train of bogie stock including milk van and Pullman car between Kilburn and Willesden Green probably around 1912. Motive power is a Westinghouse equipped loco of 1906 origin built by the Metropolitan Amalgamated Carriage & Wagon Co at Saltley.

British Westinghouse and these had a central cab flanked by lower level equipment compartments which sloped away towards the ends of the vehicle. The bodies were each mounted on a pair of motor-bogies, all wheels being motored; the motors produced a combined nominal output of 800 horsepower but were ventilated and could be significantly overrun, at least for a while. Nevertheless they were only designed to achieve a maximum speed of 36mph on the level. The locomotives, which weighed 50 tons, gave a certain amount of trouble and were the subject of some significant modifications. In 1907 ten further locomotives were ordered from BTH, but these had a cab at each end and a box-body between; these weighed about 47 tons and the four motors produced a total of about 850 horsepower. The locos were used to haul through GWR trains from Paddington to the City and from the M&GC Joint line to Baker Street (and later the City) as well. All locos were fitted with both vacuum and Westinghouse air brakes to be compatible with any trains with which they were likely to come into contact (all the electric stock then had air brakes).

In 1910 circumstances conspired to cause the Met to have the twin problem of insufficient motor coaches on the one hand and bogie stock of obsolescent design competing with lavish Great Central carriages on the other. Ingeniously, it opted to 'convert' ten of the 1905 first class trailers into a modern design of compartment carriage, creating two new loco hauled trains of what became known as 'Dreadnought' stock. Judging this design as a success, four similar (but not identical) trains were built from new in 1912. All these trains were initially arranged in 5-car sets of three 3rd-class and two 1st-class carriages having a combined seating capacity of 314. Each carriage had a 51ft 5ins body and for the first time on new such trains had passenger alarm handles fitted, though surprisingly Pintsch gas lighting prevailed for the moment, rejuvenated with an improved burner; Stone's electric lighting was substituted in 1918. First-class carriages were divided into seven compartments with 4-each-side seating of plush moquette (non-smoking compartments) or buffalo hide covering (smoking). Third class carriages were divided into three vestibules, each of which was subdivided into three interconnected semi-compartments linked centrally and separated one from the next by 2-abreast high-backed seats (with hat racks above) which did not reach the ceilings.

One of the BTH equipped locomotives in the south siding at Wembley Park station. As with the Westinghouse locomotives the bodies were built at Saltley.

The rolling stock in use on the Met main line was constantly changing as a result of its commitments to the service on the Circle Line and this (and the experimentation with prototype vehicles) perpetually caused minor changes to overall stock use and some unusual formations to supplement the main fleet. One such example was the pressing into service of a number of 'Jubilee' coaches between 1909 and 1913; arranged as three 9-carriage sets they were used on local journeys but hauled by electric locomotive. Unusually they were also fitted with shoe-beams to take current for electric lighting and heating, but they had no traction equipment.

During the 1880s and 1890s housebuilding proceeded rapidly between Kilburn and Willesden, and a little beyond; to some extent this was fuelled by the Metropolitan Railway's own housebuilding activities on its surplus land, much of which was bought for just this purpose. To facilitate improved services south of Willesden Green a bay line was commissioned on 4th January 1906 on the north side, formed by conversion of the southbound platform into an island. A goods loop was installed beyond this, for which the bay road also acted as an engine run-round.

The scale of housing development created a need for a new station between Willesden Green and Kingsbury-Neasden, to be known as Dollis Hill, which opened on 1st October 1909. This station was built with an island platform and a ticket hall beneath, with subways leading to Gladstone Park and Chapter Road (though the latter did not open until December).

In response to demand, actual or potential, the Met adopted a low-cost type of station described as a 'halt' (sometimes contemporaneously spelt 'halte'). Generally this comprised a pair of wooden platforms each with small shelter, linked by open-air footpath (with steps provided as needed) to the street and with a booking hut near to the entrance on the London-bound side. In this form Preston Road had opened on 21st May 1908 following local pressure from among others the Uxendon shooting club. Halts on the Uxbridge branch appeared at Ickenham (25th September 1905), Eastcote and Rayners Lane (26th May 1906), Ruislip Manor (5th August 1912) and West Harrow (17th November 1913). On the Joint line the long sections were broken up with a new halt at Sandy Lodge from 9th May 1910 (mainly serving the golf course) and North Harrow from 22nd March 1915. Two more stations were added in 1923, Northwick Park opening on 28th June and Hillingdon on 10th December. The former was situated between Preston Road and Harrow and served the rapidly developing area of Kenton (already served by the London, Midland & Scottish Railway and the Underground Group) and comprised an island platform with ticket hall beneath and subways to each side of the railway (although the south side was then just fields). Hillingdon, between Uxbridge and Ickenham, was completed in an enlarged form of the halt style.

To keep up with the improved service possibilities brought about by electrification, automatic signalling had been introduced between Baker Street and Finchley Road on 13th November 1910, and during 1911 had been extended all the way to Neasden & Kingsbury (as Kingsbury-Neasden had become in 1910). This helped matters to a degree and had allowed the closure of the signal boxes at Marlborough Road, Swiss Cottage, Kilburn and Dollis Hill. Signal boxes were retained elsewhere to control crossovers and sidings, though Willesden Green was comprehensively resignalled at the same time. All signals on this section were now controlled by direct current track circuits, including those where signal boxes were retained and where the levers now controlled the signals through electrical contact breakers rather than mechanical wires.

The halt at Ickenham was about as basic a station as one could get, but adequate for the sparse traffic offering. Although the platforms were only long enough for three coaches, longer trains were sometimes run which required staff to be careful to ensure nobody got out from the carriages that were not alongside.

Further stimulation was given to new traffic by the limited re-introduction of through services east of Baker Street to the City in 1909. This was inevitably very restricted until a double line connection could be restored in 1912 (as part of station reconstruction) whence many of the trains were extended to Liverpool Street and Aldgate during the peaks. When the works at Baker Street were completed there were four tracks (with a platform between each pair), the outer ones being bay roads and the centre pair through; a new all-electric signal box was commissioned on 5th January 1913 (replaced in 1924). While the new layout at Baker Street was quite adequate for a while it was a compromise which ultimately proved awkward. Ideally the terminating tracks would have been between rather than athwart the through roads, so reducing the conflicting train movements by half for each reversing train (Aldgate had long since been altered from a layout similar to Baker Street's for that very reason). Unfortunately the existing position of the sharply curved double-track tunnel to the Inner Circle was very difficult to alter. In later years the layout at Baker Street was to become the main restriction on future service development and a constant cause of service unreliability.

Despite all the new signalling the rising traffic still put the capacity of the tracks south of Wembley Park under some considerable pressure. The immediate solution was to provide a further pair of tracks south of Wembley, principally for the use of the outer suburban fast services which were prone to delay amongst the all-stations trains. It was judged very difficult to duplicate the Finchley Road tunnels, but with improvements at Baker Street and Finchley Road, and with the automatic signalling, it was felt that the railway could cope without this extravagance. The two new tracks were built on the north side of the existing line from a point just south of Finchley Road station to a point just south of Wembley Park (which already had four tracks) and the necessary powers were obtained during 1912.

This view of Baker Street station shows the two bay roads on the eastern side prior to station reconstruction in 1912. The soldiers are standing where, today, the track for platform 4 lies. In the other bay stands a train of 1905 electric saloon stock.

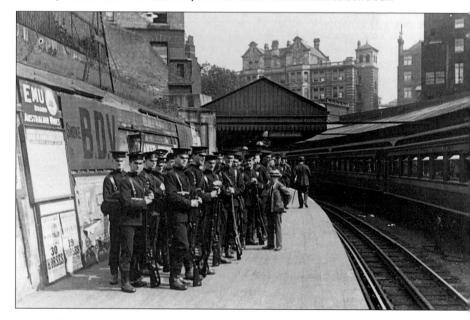

Work actually began in February 1912 (before powers had been granted), and on 30th November 1913 the new lines were opened between Finchley Road and a temporary junction just south of Kilburn. South of Finchley Road station the twin single-bore tunnels had been opened out and replaced by a new covered way, large enough to accommodate a double junction from which point the new 'fast' lines originated. At Finchley Road station itself the limited width for the new works required the old platforms to be swept away and replaced by one wide new island platform, serving what were now the 'local' lines; the fast lines passed by on the north side. A new station building was constructed at the same time, with entrances in Canfield Gardens and Finchley Road, with space available for commercial letting. At West Hampstead the new lines passed to the north of the existing tracks, requiring the West End Lane bridge to be lengthened. Towards Kilburn they rose steeply onto the widened viaduct structures, or new structures of their own.

The next section to open was that between Willesden Green and Neasden from 5th January 1914. At both these stations additional platforms were provided on the fast lines, with the result that the existing 'up' or southbound tracks became islands and new southbound 'fast' platforms were needed. As mentioned previously, at Willesden Green the old southbound platform had already been converted into an island, the other face of which had served as a bay road; the complication here was shoe-horning the new southbound 'fast' platform face into the space between the goods loop (which became the southbound fast line) and the adjacent Station Parade, and rearranging all the goods yard connections at the north end of the station. At Dollis Hill the new tracks skirted the existing station on the north side, though just at the London end of the station a massive spoil dump was created in line with the existing high level of the Willesden Green goods yard, of which it was presumably viewed as a possible future extension. At Neasden the new platforms were put in and the station re-arranged, including the addition of a novel ferro-concrete footbridge. Few alterations were made at street level at any of these stations. A week later the four tracking was continued to Wembley Park, which already had four platforms, though considerable track alterations were made and new tracks were laid to allow empty stock to proceed to and from Neasden Works. Because of the location of the Works, the 4-tracking was undertaken on the south side between Neasden and Wembley, the new tracks becoming the local lines.

The final section to be commissioned was the section between Willesden Green and a point south of Kilburn & Brondesbury where the works were most extensive. In particular two impressive steel bridges, one at Iverson Road of 99ft span, and another across Kilburn High Road of 147ft span. The latter bridge meant re-arranging the entrance to Kilburn station, which was built into the northern bridge abutment. The new lines, which came into use on 31st May 1915, were not provided with platforms at Kilburn, and the existing arrangements at platform level were retained. The new booking hall was not completed until June 1916.

Following electrification the most prominent station rebuilding scheme was at Baker Street. Although improvements had been made in the 1890s, the miserable building serving Baker Street (East) had little changed from that intended to deal with the St John's Wood Railway and was hardly fitting for the traffic carried at the turn of the century. Furthermore the separate Inner Circle entrances were in the way of a road improvement scheme so something had to be done. The 1912 re-organisation at platform level also required significant changes to the means of access. What was initially decided upon was a new main ticket hall sitting beneath an imposing street frontage, and in turn (because of the nature of the triangular site) the adoption of nearly the whole of the area for railway use. Prior to then much of the block was in residential ownership, and the Frances Holland girls school was also in the way.

Property purchase had begun as long previously as 1902 but construction work only began in 1910. The intention was to erect a 400ft frontage along the Marylebone Road behind an elevated approach road, and continued by means of 70ft returns along upper Baker Street and Allsop Place. The higher levels of the building were at first intended to be a 650-bed hotel to be run by Strand Hotel Ltd (a subsidiary of J Lyons & Co) and plans proceeded accordingly, the Met's architect producing a completed scheme for an 11-storey building. The most urgent matter was the new ticket hall to serve the revised platform arrangements and to this end the approach road and a 200ft section of the ground floor elevation was constructed forthwith, with the new ticket hall built underneath.

Much of the first phase of the work was completed during 1912. The frontage itself was of Portland stone, hiding the steel framework designed to carry the future building above. The frontage consisted of a number of arches, two occupied by sets of steps linked to the new ticket hall, one for entry and one for exit. Other arches included an enlarged parcels office and road access to a new parcels yard. The ticket hall included booking office, refreshment rooms, cloakroom, left luggage and lost property offices, bookshop and ladies waiting room.

Behind this structure a new 4-storey head office building was built fronting onto Allsop Place and with the rear wings projecting over the tracks. The new offices were ready in 1914 and were designed in 'neo-Greek' style in concrete with a faience facing, fronting Allsop Place. In later years an adjacent building (one of the Cornwall Mansion blocks) was also gradually occupied by Met staff who soon overflowed from the grand new building. There was additional accommodation for staff and passengers at platform

Ruislip and Uxbridge stations were the only ones on the Harrow & Uxbridge Railway when it opened in 1904 and both stations were very similar except that Ruislip (shown here under construction amidst green fields) required a footbridge while at Uxbridge the buildings were on the 'down' side. Dennis Edwards' collection

level. With foresight, but little ongoing determination, the station design allowed for a much needed lower level platform which would form part of a flying junction from the 'down' Inner Circle to the 'down' Met, part of which was built beneath platforms 1 and 2. At street level the original entrances were removed as the platforms were now served by the new station, but a Portland stone kiosk by the Baker Street road junction was built for an auxiliary entrance to both platforms together with a new bridge over the platforms at their western end.

With war intervening the hotel scheme did not proceed and the site lay derelict and became overgrown. In 1923, as part of the preparation for Wembley Exhibition traffic, a small ticket hall was built on the south side of Marylebone Road linking in to the bridge across the Inner Circle to the main station, and in 1924 a canopy was built over the approach road, but not much else happened. After considering a department store, the Met settled on the construction of a block of flats, but using essentially the same frontage design which by now had gained some favour. This time the theme was extended along upper Baker Street to the Bakerloo Line station about half way along, and up Allsop Place to a point near the head office building. Construction began in 1927 with the first flats ready for occupation in 1929, H. G. Wells being among the first tenants (a plaque commemorating this event was affixed to the building on 8th May 2002). By 1930 the building (named Chiltern Court, though Chequers Court was contemplated) was essentially complete with a wide range of 180 rented flats and suites available, each complete with its own unobtrusive jewel safe. During the Second World War both the station canopy and the east wing were badly damaged; the former was removed and the latter rebuilt in 1960 as a separate building in a more modern style and named Farley Court. Given the erection of further flats (Chalfont Court) over the widened tunnel mouth at the northern end of the site, the Met presided over a considerable residential development.

Harrow-on-the-Hill became the most important station outside London. The original focus was on the south (the Hill) side, as this photo shows, aiming towards the village. Later development of the Greenhill area made the north side more dominant.
LT Museum

The Heyday of Metroland

Shortly after the end of the First World War a proposal for a massive trade exhibition was seized upon, and by 1920 a government guarantee was forthcoming to fund what had become regarded as an essential tool for post-war industrial resurgence. A substantial tranche of the Wembley Park Estate land was identified, including the hill on which the disastrous Wembley Tower works had been located; indeed this precise point was to be in the centre of a gigantic sports stadium – first used for the Football Association cup final on 28th April 1923.

To the Met the Wembley Exhibition and Stadium were to be a godsend, and promised considerable future traffic potential. By way of response, a new island platform was constructed just south of the road bridge at Wembley Park, together with a dedicated ticket hall and bridge leading into the exhibition grounds. The special station was operationally well placed for the new fast lines to handle non-stop trains towards London. The existing station was also considerably modified, with extension and realignment of platforms (including provision of electric lighting and illuminated train indicators), enlargement of stairs and a rebuilt ticket hall. The British Empire Exhibition lasted for two seasons, during 1924 and 1925, and was subsequently dismantled. The stadium, however, remained, and continued to provide facilities for an eclectic selection of events, including the annual football cup final for which the Underground was an essential ingredient of its ongoing success.

The British Empire Exhibition resulted in a special station to the south of the road bridge. Equipped with its own ticket offices and pathway to the exhibition, the two new platforms were well placed to deal with the succession of fast trains to and from London.

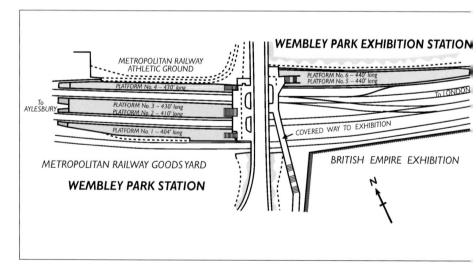

Among the other benefits of the Exhibition and its expected traffic was the provision of an additional substation at Willesden Green, in the middle of a long and busy 4-track section. At Wembley Park, as well as numerous station alterations, nine lay-by sidings were put in at the north end on the 'up' side; a government surplus shed was purchased in 1926 to cover them over. The goods yard at Wembley also benefited, so much so that it required two more roads to help deal with construction traffic.

The period after the First World War saw two major developments on the Met, electrification and resignalling between Harrow and Rickmansworth and a new branch line serving Watford. Even without the new branch there would probably have been a case for electrification to Northwood or Rickmansworth as housing began to develop in the area; the construction of the Watford line (and anticipated much-increased train service) brought matters to a head. The improvements also included the construction of a flying junction at Harrow so that the Uxbridge services could dive under the joint line without conflicting movements; this was intended to alleviate some of the concerns of the LNER about congestion caused by the new Watford branch. Harrow station had already been increased from two to four platforms in 1908 by construction of a pair of new tracks on the east side and conversion of the 'up' platform into an island. This greatly facilitated the working of the increasing services but the tracks converged north of the station for about a quarter mile before the Uxbridge branch junction. What was now planned was to extend the tracks from the newer platforms further north and take them under the original line. The flyunder came into use on 14th October 1925 though all the works there, including extensive resignalling, were not completed until the following year. A direct line was also put in between the down main and the down Uxbridge branch, intended further to reduce conflicting moves.

The joint line between Harrow and Rickmansworth was fully electrified with effect from 5th January 1925, power being supplied from Neasden via new substations at Watford Road (now Croxleyhall) and Northwood, and with Harrow enlarged to 4MW. The extension of electrification allowed the locomotive change point to be moved from Harrow to Rickmansworth, and sidings were installed on the down side just north of the platforms in which the steam engines could lay over. Since the station was only two track (and inconveniently on a curve) conditions were hardly ideal for loco changing, but it continued to take place there for another 35 years.

Even before the First World War, Watford was a sizeable place and the local authority sought to interest the Met in serving the town, though the latter was not enthusiastic. By 1911 the Met began to take the view that Watford was capable of supporting new railway facilities beyond those already provided or planned by the LNWR (at that time it was in the throes of building additional electric lines between London and Watford Junction). Accordingly parliamentary approval was obtained for a Met branch line to Watford in their Act of 1912. The line was to have terminated near the centre of town with a passenger station on Hempstead Road, near the north end of the High Street; unfortunately, Watford Urban District Council which had previously put so much pressure on the Met to build the line, was gripped with fear that such a station would involve approach lines which would ruin their beautiful Cassiobury Park, however convenient it might be for passengers. To maintain their support the line was cut back half a mile to the site of the proposed goods station in Cassiobury Park Avenue. In consequence the railway found itself stranded at the edge of town, its route firmly blocked by the park. The branch was intended to leave the main line between Sandy Lodge and Rickmansworth, and reflecting the necessary involvement of the GCR a Watford Joint Railway Committee was formed to further the project.

After the enforced delay of the First World War the Met wanted to push forward to Watford, notwithstanding the circumspection of the GCR whose financial position was less than strong and who sought without very much success to reduce the scope of works. Construction began at the end of 1922 (having received some government support) and involved a number of major earthworks including very deep cuttings and a substantial viaduct. The branch began with a triangular junction with the main line that allowed trains from Watford to proceed towards either London or Rickmansworth, where a bay platform was provided for a shuttle train to reverse. The intermediate station, Croxley Green, had two 420ft side platforms and a goods yard on the up side, while at Watford there was a 620ft island platform (with engine run rounds for each of the two tracks) and a substantial goods yard. Both station buildings were spacious and had small forecourts and parcels facilities. A new Watford Joint Committee was established (known as the Met&LNE Railways Watford Joint Committee) and this was operated on a similar basis to the Met&GC, though legally it was quite a separate body. (It might perhaps be noted here that the GCR had been absorbed by the new London & North Eastern Railway from 1st January 1923, but this did not alter the statutory title of the Met&GC).

The Watford branch opened amidst much ceremony on 2nd November 1925 with frequent through trains to both Baker Street (electric) and Marylebone (steam), and an electric shuttle to Rickmansworth. This over-capacity was hopeless and the general strike of 1926 conveniently put paid to the through Marylebone trains for good. Since the station was nowhere near the town and the area itself was under-developed, Watford was never exactly over-used and only Met-sponsored bus services that conveyed people to and from the town centre encouraged even modest use. Goods traffic was helpful and gave the LNER a valuable inroad into the area.

Increasing train services began to affect reliability on the two-track section between Wembley and Harrow-on-the-Hill, where 4-tracking was now required. The Met

Watford station's location in a suburban side street was so far from the town centre that, in an attempt to lure custom, a connecting bus was run, with a circular route via Cassiobury Park Avenue, Cassio Road, St Marys Road, Vicarage Road and Queens Avenue. The commodious station never succeeded in this objective but goods traffic was valuable and the goods yard enormous. LT Museum

An electrical multiple unit train composed of assorted saloon coaches, 1905 motor car leading and 1921 trailer adjoining. Taken near West Hampstead in the late 1920s, the Metropolitan Railway goods yard is visible in the background.

decided to build the two new lines, authorised by the Metropolitan Railway Act of 1929, in response to rapidly rising demand from housebuilding in the emerging suburbs of Pinner, Northwood and Ruislip; these were commissioned in 1931. This time the southern pair (next to the GCR line) became the fast tracks, whilst the (new) northern pair became the slow lines, which were to serve Preston Road and Northwick Park stations. One disadvantage of this arrangement was that it had the practical effect that the fast trains had to cross the slow lines on the level at Wembley Park station, which was hardly calculated to improve train running.

A necessary consequence of these works was the reconstruction of Preston Road station on a new site north of the road bridge, an island platform being provided leading up to a smart new ticket hall at street level. At Northwick Park the comparatively new island platform had to be shifted sideways both to serve and make room for the new

Rebuilt electric loco heading north on the fast lines past West Hampstead with train of Dreadnought coaches and Pullman Car. Just visible in front of the footbridge is one of the automatic semaphore signals used in the open air electrified area. During the 1938 track rearrangement the platforms were rebuilt further to the left (to a point abutting the train). LT Museum

tracks; they extended to a point just south of Harrow-on-the-Hill station which was otherwise unaltered. Improved services to Harrow meant improvements beyond as well, especially on the Uxbridge branch, which was developing rapidly. However there was only a single substation on this line (at Ruislip, near Ickenham) and a second was opened at Eastcote from 3rd March 1930 using second-hand equipment. Neasden substation was also supplemented with equipment displaced from elsewhere.

Power generation requirements at Neasden had inevitably risen. From 1908 an additional turbine rated at 5MW was introduced, together with additional boilers and other enhancements, and after the rewinding of the older turbines the station had an installed output of 25MW until the 1920s. Major reconstruction in the early 1920s facilitated the installation of a further generator and not inconsiderable associated plant, providing an additional 12.5MW capacity and by 1923, ready for the Rickmansworth electrification, the station had a capacity of roundly 35MW. More improvements in 1926 brought the station up to the capacity then needed to supply sufficient power for the new electrification; this consisted of the replacement of one of the original 5MW generators by a new one of 15MW, together with other associated improvements. This process was repeated in 1928 when another old unit was replaced by a 20MW unit, and again in 1931 and 1937 with two further 20MW units (both of which could operate under 25 per cent overload conditions). A very considerable amount of associated plant was required including a fourth artesian well and much additional cooling apparatus.

The Met had kept a weather eye on the developing area north of Wembley Park, lying roughly mid-way between its own line to Harrow and the Underground Group's Edgware branch, opened in 1924 (and which charged artificially low fares). Towards the end of the 'twenties housing development seemed inevitable; the Canons Park estate was for sale, and everywhere in the neighbourhood house builders were applying pressure for improved transport facilities to help unlock their fortunes.

The Met was nervous about the limited capacity south of Finchley Road to carry general traffic increases even without another branch line feeding traffic. It was just as nervous about getting a decent financial return from a line into as yet undeveloped country. In 1929 a government guarantee for the necessary capital was forthcoming for both the branch and other capacity relieving measures and it was in this climate that the decision to build a Stanmore branch was taken.

The necessary works for the branch were authorised in the Met's 1930 Act, and work started in November of that year. It was to be just over four miles long from its junction with the new 'local' lines half a mile to the north of Wembley Park station from which point it was to curve sharply north-west. The terminus at Stanmore was situated about half a mile from the village centre. Intermediate stations were built at Kingsbury Green and Canons Park (Edgware), though at opening the former was actually named 'Kingsbury' (Neasden and Kingsbury station lost the suffix at the same time). Provision was also made for a third station between Kingsbury and Canons Park, contrived to be called 'Queensbury' though this was not immediately proceeded with. The Stanmore branch opened on 10th December 1932. At Stanmore itself a small goods yard was built, and a new substation at Canons Park supplied power from Neasden, together with another new substation near the junction (called Preston Road).

Stanmore and Kingsbury stations were designed by the Met's architect C. W. Clark in a similar 'cottage' style to that adopted on the Watford line; these were of red brick structure with a large pitched roof accommodating an apartment which could be let out to staff. At Canons Park the line crossed over the road and the ticket hall was built into the bridge abutment.

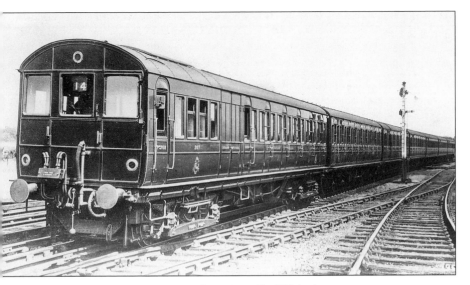

An MV Stock train of 1927 origin shortly after delivery. The MV stock was vacuum braked and similar but slightly later cars, designated MW stock, employed the Westinghouse air brake.

Two years after opening it was noted that the three shuttle and three 'through' trains per hour to Stanmore were 'in no way taxed' and that whilst building development had been slow (largely because of poor road access), there was vigorous activity in the Kingsbury area. The design of stations caused some reflection and it was wondered if they had perhaps blended in a little too harmoniously with the surroundings, to the detriment of attracting new traffic. The fares levels were clearly causing some difficulty. The Met had been charging fares on the main line railway scale, with the result that the fare from (say) Stanmore to Moorgate was 1s 3d (6p), compared with 7d (3p) from nearby Edgware; it was drily observed that for this reason the sparse feeder bus services were actually drawing traffic away! It was recommended amongst other things that the fares be brought down (achieved in 1936), better publicity be provided, including bullseye signs, and that a car park be provided at Stanmore.

The work of line quadrupling and the opening to Stanmore also involved provision of a fifth platform (today's platform 5) within the main station at Wembley Park, built at the back of the up fast platform which was converted into an island. This was intended to provide a bay road for the Stanmore shuttle service to reverse in, as well as increase general manoeuvring space; doubtless it would also have helped out at times when trains were going out of service at Wembley to go to the depot at Neasden, and it became the main road for access into and out of Wembley Park shed (reduced to seven roads by the building of the additional lines to Harrow). These changes meant the island 'Exhibition' platform south of the station was now in the way, requiring demolition and replacement in 1931 by a single platform linked by steps to the former street level buildings. This maintained a segregated facility for football traffic, though it seems not to have been heavily used. It was finally demolished in 1937 as part of yet further improvements.

With increasing traffic levels it became obvious that some of the inner suburban stations were inadequate. At street level the degenerating facilities at St John's Wood Road were much improved from October 1925 when a rebuilt structure was completed. This had a more prominent frontage; it was finished in cream faience tiling characteristic of the period and had space for commercial letting. The remainder of the station was improved and tiled at the same time. Willesden Green was reconstructed during the same period and the commodious street level frontage completed in September 1925. Swiss Cottage also received treatment. Here a new frontage on to the Finchley Road was provided as part of a shopping arcade, and the remainder of the station modernised; the work was completed in September 1929. All these works were designed by Clark in faience tiled style.

At platform level there was a need to accommodate at least 7-coach trains on the electrified lines between Baker Street and Uxbridge, and in the event facilities allowed for eight coaches at most locations. The work was authorised by an Act of 1929, and completed between 1930 and 1932. At the open-air stations there was, of course, little difficulty in extending platforms. Along the north side of the Circle between Great Portland Street and Aldgate, much of the line was in tunnel or cutting where the problems were significant and involved considerable expenditure. At Marlborough Road and Swiss Cottage platform lengthening was planned but in the end such expense was viewed as quite unwarranted and extensions in the form of narrow wooden catwalks were all that were provided; St John's Wood was a little easier as one end was in the open air. This breezy approach had its problems. At Swiss Cottage the catwalk on the down (northbound) line was entirely at the southern end where there wasn't

The rebuilt St John's Wood station, one of a number of similarly faced structures designed for the met by C. W. Clark. LT Museum

44

This view of a remarkably tidy station at Aylesbury shows a Metropolitan train in the bay road consisting of 'Dreadnought' carriages hauled by a 'G' class 0-6-4 tank. The line to Verney Junction lies straight on.

really the room. At over 120ft long and generally no more than 2ft 9ins wide both platform staff and guards had to ensure passengers were clear before trains could be allowed to start, notwithstanding three refuges. This did nothing for punctuality and was an open invitation for disaster. A few years later a passage from the end of the proper platform had to be tunnelled behind the catwalk, together with seven openings, so the catwalk could be serviced by an opening never more than a few feet away – surely a unique arrangement.

Some of the outer stations were soon to outgrow their halt status. At North Harrow housing development was rapid and required the construction of a proper station building and better access road, completed in 1931. A permanent station building was constructed behind the bridge support, with an entrance each side tiled in Clarke's cream faience. While designed and built by the Met, the work was necessarily on behalf of the Met&GC Joint Committee whose title (since chiselled off) appeared in the tilework over the entrances. The station name appeared in the Met's 'stencil' style over the entrances, surprisingly one of these surviving until very recently as a unique example of this once common style until it was unceremoniously scrapped. At platform level, little was changed and though the wooden structures were enlarged they remain today as the last example of this type of construction. At other halts it was necessary to lengthen the shorter platforms, and Sandy Lodge became Moor Park & Sandy Lodge to reflect to arrival of a new housing estate.

Improving the longer distance services required more powerful traction than the fleet of small and ageing tank locomotives could supply on their own. From 1915 four new 0-6-4 tank locomotives entered service; each was built by the Yorkshire Engine Company and was substantially heavier than anything previously operated by the Met.

Its 3-piece brass nameplate shining brightly, this view of Metropolitan Vickers loco No 9 was photographed at Neasden in its final Metropolitan Railway livery. Just visible by the leading cab window is a wing mirror with which these locomotives were fitted.

During 1920–21 eight large 4-4-4 tanks entered service; built by Kerr Stewart these were intended predominantly to take over the longer passenger train workings. Finally, in 1925, a further six tanks entered service. These were constructed by Armstrong Whitworth as 2-6-4 tanks from unused parts built during the war for intended 2-6-0 tender locomotives; they were the most powerful machines available on the Met and were normally employed on freight work. The arrival of this new motive power meant that many of the older locomotives could be scrapped.

By 1919 the existing electric locomotives were clearly underpowered compared with the prevailing electric stock and it was intended to rebuild them with modern and more powerful equipment of Metropolitan Vickers origin so that improved non-stop services could be operated. After an experimental rebuild of number 17 it was found that in practice it would be simpler to construct new bodies and scrap the old ones, with minimal reuse of a few parts. The locomotives were all delivered in the period 1921–23 and each had a total power rating of 1200 horsepower and a maximum speed of 60mph. The prototype locomotive demonstrated several minor shortcomings that were put right and adopted for the production batch. Being the first, and for a while the most photographed machine, it was number 17 which almost invariably appeared on subsequent Met publicity. In 1927 it was decided to name the locomotives after notables reputed to have had some association with the Met's area, and smart bronze nameplates were prepared. Two particular variations to this theme were number 15 which had appeared at the Wembley exhibition in 1925, and became, a little misleadingly, *Wembley 1924* and number 8 which became *Sherlock Holmes*, who, though living in the area, did so on a purely fictitious basis. It may be complete co-incidence but the first locomotive actually to appear named in service was the ever-present number 17, which became *Florence Nightingale*, emerging on 3rd October 1927. It was over a year before they were all named, including *Wembley 1924* whose nameplates were surmounted by a small bronze lion, the emblem of the exhibition.

Ever since the arrival of the GCR the Met struggled to compete in terms of comfort and appearance. In seeking to upgrade quality one of the innovations it had introduced was a Pullman car service in 1910. An agreement was reached with the Pullman Car Company for the construction of two special vehicles for use on the Met system; the vehicles were nearly 60ft long, the longest to operate regular services, requiring minor track adjustments. Named *Mayflower* and *Galatea*, they could each accommodate nineteen passengers in two large and one small private saloon, furnished with plush leather armchairs with tables and reading lamps; both carriages had lavatories and a small pantry from which refreshments (including breakfast) could be served by the attendant whose attention could be attracted by an electric bell at each table. The carriages were normally worked separately and were marshalled in the centre of certain formations. They were available to first class passengers and a Pullman supplement of one shilling was charged during most of their lives (or sixpence if the car was used only south of Rickmansworth). Both carriages were finished in the standard Pullman colours of umber and cream, but in later years were painted crimson lake as the cream did not wear well, the only Pullmans to have been so treated. The key working were on two up trains in the morning which returned in the evening peak, and a late night down train for those who had spent the evening out.

By the late 1920s train services had developed considerably from those of twenty years earlier; the most notable changes had been a significant increase in the inner area frequencies and the abandonment of any real attempt to develop traffic north of Aylesbury. Off peak frequencies were not exactly of the regular 'clock-face' pattern but more or less resolved themselves into half-hour services from both Watford and Uxbridge that ran fast south of Wembley Park. There was also a half-hour all-stations service from Rayners Lane with a considerable number of additional trains starting at either Wembley Park or Neasden & Kingsbury to produce a combined all-stations service of around 4–5 minute intervals, though only the Rayners Lane and Wembley Park trains stopped at Marlborough Road and St John's Wood Road. Nearly all trains terminated at Baker Street, though, unaccountably, every half-hour one of the Neasden trains worked through to Aldgate.

There were only two through trains a day from Verney Junction (both in the afternoon) with what passed for the remainder of the service being operated by a local train as far as Aylesbury where through passengers had to change. Most of the off-peak Aylesbury–London trains worked to Marylebone. A shuttle train ran between Watford and Rickmansworth about every 20 minutes, the journey taking only six minutes.

In the rush hours things were a bit more complicated. Slightly more than half the trains worked through to Moorgate, Liverpool Street or Aldgate; intervals from the outer stations were reduced to very roughly 20 minutes from Watford and more frequently (but very unevenly) from Uxbridge. Through trains operated from Quainton Road or Aylesbury to the City, and with the local trains from Wembley Park and Neasden, intervals approaching Baker Street were averaging about one train every 2½ to 3 minutes.

With the more intensive electric working required by resumption of through services to the City and the new fast lines to Wembley, some additional rolling stock was needed. Some 23 motor coaches and 20 trailers were ordered in 1913 with enclosed end vestibules fitted with sliding doors, and a central doorway (also fitted with sliding doors). The coaches were all open saloon vehicles, motor coaches all third class and trailers divided equally into firsts and thirds. These cars operated mostly but not exclusively on the Inner Circle and could be interworked with the older stock.

An electric multiple unit train, 1921 stock car trailing, leaving Harrow-on-the-Hill around 1924, just prior to colour light signalling being commissioned.

From 1920 a further delivery of steam stock was made (seven 6-carriage trains, but the design hadn't changed much since 1912) following which the remaining nineteenth century bogie stock was available for alternative use; a further 20 carriages (the final batch) emerged in 1923. During the same period a further 59 electric vehicles were also purchased to a design similar to the 1913 cars except that the trailers had three pairs of double doors per car side (instead of one central double door and two singles at the ends). The order comprised 20 motor coaches and 33 trailers (all third class) and six driving trailers (first class). Amongst the various odds, ends, conversions and experiments which would characterise any more comprehensive a story of the Met's complex rolling stock might perhaps be mentioned a single first class trailer of '1921' stock built specially for display at the British Empire Exhibition in 1924 and thereafter put into service. The influx of the Dreadnought stock allowed all the locomotive hauled services to be of the latest type of train and the remaining 'bogie' stock vehicles were all converted to electric working.

Following electrification to Rickmansworth, and the opening to Watford, a further need for new rolling stock arose which caused two prototypes to be constructed. Amongst other things, these demonstrated quite clearly a preference by Metropolitan Railway passengers for compartment-type vehicles on the longer distance services, the means of haulage being irrelevant (a conclusion also reached by the Southern Railway who, like the Met, also noted that boarding and alighting was faster with compartment stock too).

Following evaluation of the prototypes some 132 vehicles were constructed between 1927 and 1931, comprising 60 motor cars and 72 trailers. The make-up was complicated because the earlier coaches (1927/29) were used either with existing trailers or with converted loco-hauled stock to produce trains which looked similar but had quite different and wholly incompatible equipment. The later coaches (1929/31) initially produced five 7-coach trains of a new type called MW stock (later increased to 8-coach trains) and then a further seven 8-coach trains which were intended to be compatible MW trains but in practice would not intermingle because of minor unforeseen incompatibilities.

The coach bodies of the earlier cars were not dissimilar to those of the 1921 coaches but arranged for nine compartments within the trailers. The earlier ones had teak bodies and varnished-teak exteriors, but the 1931 cars were covered in steel sheets which were painted in a brown stipple to look like teak. The motor coaches had the equipment mounted behind the driver, disposed centrally with a gangway each side; this left room for six passenger compartments.

One of the justifications for the Met's north-western expansion was the ability to develop freight business, though this grew quite slowly. The original St John's Wood Railway was expressly prohibited from carrying goods, and authority to do so was only obtained in 1873 when extension was imminent. When Harrow was reached in 1880 the first coal handling facilities were provided, and exchange sidings with the Midland Railway at Finchley Road offered a convenient outlet for the goods traffic. Met-owned goods and coal facilities subsequently emerged at Finchley Road (1894), Neasden (1894), Wembley Park (1894), and Willesden Green (1899). The arrival of the Great Central Railway provided a northerly goods outlet that further increased traffic potential, and the LNWR at Verney Junction was another valuable connection. Several yards were increased in size over the years, notably at Willesden Green where considerable milk traffic was dealt with (the Met had even built special milk carrying vehicles). At most of the later stations goods yards were generally provided when the station opened, exceptions being at Dollis Hill, North Harrow and Sandy Lodge. At West Hampstead, which only ever aspired to a siding, freight handling became merged with the expanded Finchley Road yard.

London goods traffic was mainly handled at Willesden Green, but this was far from perfect as goods had frequently to be forwarded nearer London by road. In 1909 some sidings at Farringdon were converted into a small goods handling facility, with compact warehouse above connected by a lift, with trucks to the yard being hauled from Finchley Road or Willesden Green by electric locomotive. The Met used various private hauliers for their short distance goods movement by road, but from 1919 undertook this activity themselves using their own vehicles, horses and staff. On the Met&GC section private haulage contractors continued until the late 1920s when in most cases Met&GC staff and vehicles were employed on this work. By 1932 the Met owned 519 goods vehicles (and 22 goods brake vans) and were handling nearly 400,000 tons of freight at Met-owned stations and 300,000 tons at joint stations.

The Met began to engage in the parcels business on the 'extension' line from 1889. This involved acceptance and storage of parcels at the stations, carriage on their trains and local delivery by road; an express parcels delivery service began in 1909. The carriage of parcels on the Met main line was an extension of the parcels service offered at the Met's inner London stations and grew to such proportions that in 1893 a parcels office was built at Baker Street employing several staff; this was rebuilt in 1913 and further extended in the 1920s.

The signalling at the time of electrification was the unchanged mechanical system inherited from the steam age regime – everything controlled by local signal boxes mainly at the stations and using the electric telegraph for communication. This was generally adequate although it proved necessary to introduce a few intermediate signal boxes on very long sections. Thus Watford Road (between Rickmansworth and Northwood) appeared in 1899, Dutchlands (between Great Missenden and Wendover) in 1900 and Mantles Wood (between Amersham and Great Missenden) in 1900, each facilitating the operation of the Great Central's trains.

After electrification the build up of traffic south of Wembley Park prompted the Met to introduce automatic signals, favourable experience of these having been gained on the Inner Circle. The all-electric installation was confined to the Baker Street–Neasden section, a distance of about five miles. The existing signal cabins were retained at St John's Wood Road (where an emergency crossover was retained until 1971), Finchley Road and West Hampstead where there were sidings at each, and Neasden where the existing signalling was retained to the north. At Willesden a new 40-lever mechanical frame was provided in a new signal box (replacing two older ones). At each of these locations the points were mechanically controlled but the signals were electrically operated and interlocked by track circuits. At the first three locations the signal boxes were arranged for completely automatic working when unmanned. All other intermediate signals were fully automatic and the signal boxes were permanently closed. The signals themselves were upper-quadrant semaphores in the open air, actuation being by electric motor which drove the arm to the 'off' position where it was retained by a magnetic latch; they returned to danger by gravity. The purely automatically operated signals bore a horizontal white stripe on the otherwise red arm. In tunnel sections 2-aspect lamp signals were used. Repeater signals were required where sighting was poor, and in the open the Met employed signals with yellow arms with a notched end and a black 'fishtail' marking, this later becoming the standard for all distant signals on British railways. The installation was commissioned in 1911 and all stop signals were equipped with automatic train stops that applied the brakes on any train passing at danger, continuing the practice adopted throughout the Inner Circle.

At Baker Street the re-opening of the Baker Street junction resulted in the East station signal box being shifted to the north end of the station. However, from 1913 a new all-electric signal box was opened (also at the north end of the station) which replaced both the existing box and a second signal box controlling the Inner Circle and the junction. This came into use on 5th January 1913 and had 30 levers (and 6 spaces). Signals were all of the colour light variety.

With the track widening to Wembley Park in 1913–15 the opportunity was taken to provide automatic signals on the new (fast) lines and to extend automatic working through Wembley Park to Harrow-on-the-Hill. This required new signal cabins at West Hampstead (normally unmanned), and Finchley Road, which was given a large cabin which also controlled the busy new junction. Two intermediate boxes were closed between Wembley Park and Harrow-on-the-Hill, which retained its mechanical controls. From 1921 Quainton Road Junction was remotely controlled from the station box using a novel form of battery operated equipment and track circuits, but there were few other changes north of Rickmansworth.

The extension of electric working to Rickmansworth required some improvement in the signalling arrangements and 3-aspect coloured lights controlled by a.c. track circuits replaced the main line semaphores between Harrow-on-the-Hill (inclusive) and Rickmansworth, though the latter retained its mechanical signal arms. Existing signal boxes were retained but, except at Harrow, all of them were normally closed except when shunting was required of goods trains, or in emergency. The new signalling came into service from 30th November 1924. Similar signalling was also introduced when the Watford branch was opened in 1925. In this instance the Watford Road signal box was replaced and arranged to operate all three junctions on the triangle, the nearest one using mechanical connections to the points and the other two with electric controls. The final section of line to be signalled automatically during this period was the Uxbridge branch, which received 3-aspect signals during 1930, again with the old signal boxes relegated to use during shunting operations only.

This view from the Dog Lane bridge shows the southern entrance to Neasden Works with the 'fast' lines to the left of the signal and the 'slow' lines to their left (with a down train in evidence). The signal box is Neasden Yard box but did not control signals on the main line. In the far distance may be seen the power house.

When the Stanmore branch was opened the signalling was quite revolutionary in this country. It was known as Centralised Traffic Control (CTC) – the only example found on the Underground. This was a form of operation where instructions from, and indications to, the signal box at Wembley Park were transmitted over a dedicated 3-wire line in code; the electrical interlocking equipment at Stanmore was therefore entirely unmanned. Intermediate signals between Wembley Park and Stanmore were 3-aspect fully automatic. The CTC controls and track circuit indications were fitted to an equipment panel in the existing signal box at Wembley Park.

In the early years of the twentieth century there emerged a number of Underground railways of a new type, electric systems built in deep level iron tubes, a mode of construction that allowed lines to be built across rather than around central London. Although they competed fiercely at first, particularly with the older systems, electrification had put all the lines on a more or less equal footing and it became clear that it was in everyone's best interest to promote travel by 'Underground' over the network as a whole. From 1908 it was therefore agreed that the Metropolitan Railway would participate in this marketing arrangement and promote the sale of through tickets and share in the promotion of certain types of maps and publicity. Most important was the display at its central London stations of signs displaying the word UNDERGROUND, but this particular facet did not affect the stations beyond the central area. In later years the Underground Group came to own all the London underground railways except the Met and the Waterloo & City, and came to introduce station name boards consisting of a red disc across which was a blue bar carrying the station name in white (later the disc was replaced by a red ring). The Met, sensing this was a good idea, adopted a similar principle based on a blue bar across a solid red diamond shape, and such signs appeared at most stations in the electrified area, including some of those on the joint lines.

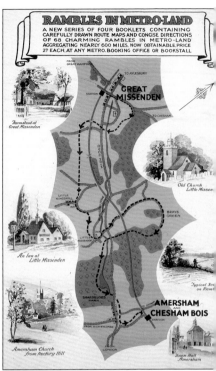

Two Metropolitan Railway posters from 1929, one for its parcels service and one advertising its Country Walks booklets. The abbreviation 'Metro' was being used by the publicity department at this time. LT Museum

After the First World War the Met was prolific in its publicity and for many years produced a wide range of imaginative posters to promote its services, of which, unfortunately, very few survive. It was famous also for its booklets promoting country walks which started in 1905. These demonstrated that traffic could be generated to remote country stations even if few people lived there; the popularity of such journeys was further increased by means of cheap tickets, such as walking tour tickets which allowed return from a different station. The Country Walks theme was also adopted by the Met&GC upon whose metals there was perhaps more scope, especially in later years when housebuilding was making 'country' walking more difficult in the Met's now built up area. In 1915 the Met started to produce a separate series of booklets known as Metro-land which covered the joint line too. This extolled the joys of the Met's countryside and in the post-war editions it became a medium for the heavy promotion of house buying in the Metro-land area. Although it carried advertisements for many of the local property developers' particular attention was given to the estates built on the Metropolitan Railway's own considerable surplus lands and those of a nominally independent but entirely controlled developer, the Metropolitan Railway Country Estates Ltd. The Met was not slow to recognise that money could be made from the land but also that by encouraging people to live in the area it would produce assured ongoing season ticket revenue.

The Met also printed a range of maps showing its services. These were rather surprising documents employing a variable scale which resulted in such peculiarities as Golders Green and Highgate being further north than Watford, Acton Town being directly due south of Quainton Road and St Albans being a little to the west of Golders Green (and closer than Hampstead!) Even more surprising was the railway's superimposition on what looked superficially like an accurate road layout. This was a novel way of dealing with the awkward problem of showing clearly the congested central London area at the same time as the wilds of Brill. These maps were produced in parallel with those pushed out by the Underground Group which did illustrate the Met but usually only as far out as about Preston Road. In early 1933 the UERL experimented with a new design of 'map' for their own underground railways, this time relying on the lines being shown in clear diagrammatic form (using 90- and 45-degree angles) rather than retaining any close geographical link. The lines of the Metropolitan Railway continued to be shown but still awkwardly because of the large geographical spread. This time the diagrammatic compression of the outer London areas allowed more of the Met to be revealed – as far out as Rickmansworth, which by logic or coincidence was the limit of electric services. All the same there was at first no clue that trains ran beyond (unlike the UERL's treatment of the eastern end of the District Line which had outer destinations listed in a box), though this was adjusted in following editions. Only from 1938 was the network shown out as far as Aylesbury.

Map issued by the Metropolitan Railway, c.1928. LT Museum

London Transport and New Works

From 1929 it became increasingly clear that the movement towards some sort of 'integrated' transport body within the London area was likely to be established, there being general cross party support for such a beast. It was to appear before the public on 1st July 1933. The London Passenger Transport Board – popularly 'London Transport' – was inevitably built upon the foundations laid by the UERL whose constituents dominated the new organisation notwithstanding the incorporation of various private buses and municipal tramways within the 1986 square mile area within which it had an effective monopoly. Of course this meant the end of the Metropolitan Railway whose directors and shareholders were paid off and the whole enterprise (less the property businesses) became a part of the new London Transport – but now named 'Metropolitan Line'. It is worth observing at this point that about half the Metropolitan Line between Baker Street and Verney Junction actually projected beyond the new London Passenger Transport Area.

Over the following years control and administration of the Metropolitan was where possible shifted from Baker Street to 55 Broadway. However the various peculiarities that marked out the Metropolitan as different (such the compartment trains, fast and stopping services, the rural areas served, the different fares structures, etc) were not at all easy to change overnight. Furthermore the Met&GC and Met&LNE joint lines carried on with their own separate legal status and more or less the only immediate thing to change was the substitution on their boards of LT representatives for those of the Metropolitan Railway. However, from 1937 LT had agreed with the Met&GC that stations to the south of Aylesbury would be staffed entirely by LT staff, and those to the north by staff of the LNER (Aylesbury itself had its own staff because of the Great Western's continued interest there; these sported caps and buttons marked AJS, for Aylesbury Joint Station). Although new staff could in theory be used elsewhere than solely on the Met&GC, the transferred staff were awarded protected status, retaining special terms and conditions and for most purposes being deployable only on the Met&GC section of line – the last of these gentlemen only retired in the 1980s.

London Transport was unenthusiastic about the conveyance of either goods or parcels traffic on its railways, notwithstanding that both had been carried on the Metropolitan for many years and thereby provided a useful service to the wider community. Being required by statute to provide only passenger services, these other trappings of railway business were regarded as a distraction. As quickly as summer 1934, LT had decided to discontinue from 2nd July the conveyance of unaccompanied luggage and parcels traffic, including collection and delivery. Arrangements were made for the main line railways to take over the business using their own trains, stations and vehicles, so far as possible. Existing Met Line parcels offices were retained (usually) as cloakroom facilities, and newspapers continued to be conveyed locally. None of this affected the Met&GC (or Met&LNE) stations, which no doubt under the heavy influence of the LNER, carried on exhibiting all the characteristics of a fully-fledged main line railway.

With London Transport as just a fifty per cent owner of Quainton Road the main line 'look and feel' carried on. This view shows a mixed train for the Brill branch waiting in the branch platform shortly before the service was withdrawn in 1935, loco 41 leading. Goods traffic was probably always more important than passenger at this remote location. LT Museum

Goods workings took a little longer to sort out. LT soon decided to close its small in-town goods station at Vine Street (Farringdon), with effect from the departure of the train on the night of 30th June 1936. More drastically, negotiations with the LNER resulted in wholesale transfer of responsibility for all local goods services to them with effect from 1st November 1937. In consequence the LNER took over all LT's main line steam locomotive and goods rolling stock, the various goods wagons, and the goods agents and their staff at the various Met and Met&GC goods yards. A by-product of this was that the responsibility for haulage of passenger trains north of Rickmansworth also became that of the LNER, although the existing locomotives carried on under their new owners for a few years, but based at Neasden LNER shed. LT retained control of a small fleet of eleven ex-Metropolitan locomotives for use on ballast trains, and at Neasden yard. It is known that at times of serious locomotive shortage the LT locomotives were occasionally still used to haul Metropolitan trains north of Rickmansworth, and there was for example such a spate of activity in 1946.

It was always inconceivable that LT would be able to overlook the highly idiosyncratic operation of the Brill branch, which soon sported vehicles carrying the words 'London Transport' on them. Nothing was new. Locomotive duties were split between two ancient 'A' class tanks of the 1860s and the main carriage was a rigid 8-wheeler, usually formed up as part of a mixed train as likely as not including farm animals. Of course, the responsibility for this line lay with the Met&GC Joint Committee so things had to be arranged through that. The Met&GC Board was persuaded during 1934 that over £2000 a year could be saved by withdrawing from the line and it advised the statutory Oxford & Aylesbury Tramroad Company (still controlled by Earl Temple) that it wished to do so immediately. The O&AT refused to acquiesce to this and it was necessary for the Met&GC to give the required notice under the terms of the original letter. The last train actually ran on 30th November 1935. Inevitably the last day generated a great number of journeys to view this peculiar outpost, but the deed was done and services ceased. However, the Met&GC, like the

Metropolitan before it, had never actually owned the line so upon closure it reverted, track, stations, appurtenances and all, to the Oxford & Aylesbury Tramroad Company which was in absolutely no position to operate any trains of its own; accordingly it could do little more than sell the track for scrap and put the whole affair up for auction by Burrows and Bradfield on 2nd April 1936. The 53 lots sold went for a total of £112 10 shillings, the cheapest items being the Westcott station sign (one shilling) and the oil lamps from the Westcott level crossing (one shilling the pair), and the most expensive items the Brill goods shed (with brick cellars) and the 37-yard long platform at Waddesden Road, both items reaching £7 10 shillings. The railway houses at Westcott and Brill were auctioned separately and raised a slightly more respectable £305 and £350 respectively. With the tramroad never having owned the freehold of the line, the trackbed gradually re-merged with the neighbouring land.

The passenger service on the Verney Junction line was the next area to receive attention, though by this time LT's presence there was, to say the least, very slight (two through Met trains a day – both in the evening – and six LNER rail-motors). Nevertheless the maintenance of passenger facilities of any sort was clearly regarded as unfathomable by LT and it was felt that even if goods services were retained it ought to have been possible to reduce the overall financial burden on the Met&GC (to which LT had to contribute). In consequence the Met&GC agreed during 1935 to withdraw passenger trains between Quainton Road and Verney Junction from 6th July 1936, even though the saving only amounted to £42 a year and there would be some demolition costs; the last train actually ran on 4th July as none ran on Sundays. Winslow Road and Granborough Road stations were closed at the same time, together with Waddesden Manor, never of outstanding use, which was formerly served by the same trains. To reduce costs further the Verney line was singled with effect from 28th January 1940 (the up line being retained) so that intermediate signal boxes could be closed: a similar idea had been considered as long previously as 1914. Two tracks remained north of Winslow Road, the second one acting as a long siding. By one of those quirks of fate, the newly-singled line became quite busy with freight transfers during the Second World War, and the LNER had no difficulty acquiescing to the construction of a second junction between the former GCR main line near Calvert and the Oxford–Bletchley line, which opened in 1940, and was part of wartime freight ring allowing trains to avoid London. Afterwards this was found to cope with all the now-depleted goods traffic and the Met&GC Quainton Road–Verney Junction line lost its freight service completely from 8th September 1947. Perhaps oddly it was mothballed for a while and track lifting only began in 1958. Little remains today, but the station at Verney Junction continued to advertise the possibilities of changing for the Metropolitan nearly until the withdrawal of passenger services on the Oxford–Bletchley line in 1967.

An early London Transport decision was to extend the Piccadilly Line service to Uxbridge over the former Metropolitan Railway. From the late 1920s plans were developed by the UERL to project the Piccadilly Line westwards from its Hammersmith terminus along the tracks of the District Railway, improving services significantly on the western branches upon which traffic was developing rapidly. However, the statutory powers which related to the District's use of the Uxbridge branch were specific to the Metropolitan District Railway and confined its use to three trains an hour. In consequence the Piccadilly Line extension was compelled to finish at South Harrow and arrangements were developed to operate a so-called 'District' shuttle between Uxbridge and South Harrow. There had been desultory discussions with the Metropolitan to do something a bit better, but to no avail. Under LT ownership everything changed and there was no longer considered to be any legal impediment to through running. From 23rd October 1933 the shuttles were abandoned and a proportion of through tube trains began to work to Uxbridge. As platforms on the Uxbridge branch were suitable for main line but not 'tube' trains they had to be adjusted to a compromise height between the two.

As traffic continued to develop it was in due course considered expedient to be able to project as far as Rayners Lane some of the trains that still reversed at South Harrow, so that ongoing passengers could use Met services. The antiquated track and signalling arrangements there were not very convenient for this and would in due course require new signalling and a western reversing siding. A new station building was also planned. Fate accelerated matters as a runaway ballast train demolished the existing signal cabin (in the angle between the two routes) in November 1934, and a year later a new track layout and signal cabin came into use. The signal cabin, this time safely parked at the west end of the station, incorporated a 35-lever power frame using the push-pull system, the first of this type on the Underground. Here the levers stood in the mid position and by pushing or pulling each one so one of two complete routes could be set up, speeding operation and reducing space needed. While the siding was not at first overworked, several Metropolitan Line trains used it throughout the day and some peak hour Piccadilly trains were extended from South Harrow to Rayners Lane in May 1936. Regular Piccadilly reversing was introduced at Rayners Lane on Sundays from October 1937, and all week from October 1943. The regular use by Metropolitan Line trains ceased in 1940. A new substation was added at Rayners Lane from 26th February 1939.

This view of Northwood in 1934 would not be untypical of many stations on the joint line. The station survived in much the same state until rebuilt in 1962. LT Museum

Another 'early win' for London Transport was the opening on 13th November 1933 of a new station at Northwood Hills, between Pinner and Northwood, a distance of about 2½ miles; this, of course, represented an initiative begun in Metropolitan Railway days. By 1931 housebuilding was proceeding in earnest in this area and the Met&GC, conscious of pressure to build a station in the area, was able to secure half the cost from local estate agents; construction was authorised in December 1932, with the design the responsibility of the Met. Another early London Transport win was Queensbury station, opened on 16th December 1934 when local building development warranted it (including development at the former Stag Lane airfield). The railway laid out some of the nearby streets, including Queensbury Circus, which is still owned by London Underground today. The Queensbury station building was comparatively large and incorporated a parade of shops with flats above.

One of the purposes of the new Board was further to develop and co-ordinate public transport facilities in London, an unenviable task given the phenomenal rate of growth of London at the time, and increasing difficulty in obtaining capital funding for much needed new works. The Board soon formulated a co-ordinated grand scheme of new works with the main line railways and obtained a government guarantee for the money needed, to be raised through a shares issue. Thus was born the 1935-40 New Works Programme, of which the Metropolitan Line to Stanmore and Amersham was to feature significantly.

The programme benefited the Met by including several much needed station reconstructions, some of them the halts that were now in busy built up areas. Rayners Lane (1938), Eastcote (1939), Ruislip Manor (1938) and Uxbridge stations were rebuilt to the latest architectural standards, though it is perhaps regrettable that the 'round-the-corner' interchange traffic at Rayners Lane was not better catered for by provision of an island platform – two long staircases have to be negotiated. At Uxbridge the station was moved considerably closer to the town centre, under powers in the 1936 LPTB Act, and a new 3-track (4-platform) structure replaced the 2-platform steam age affair on 4th December 1938. As part of this work a new substation opened on the same date and rolling stock sidings were added near the old station (though they were not completed until 1942). Stations were all of light brick facing though concrete is evident in some quantity. Effort was made to keep spaces open and airy and free-standing ticket-issuing booths were provided rather than more traditional wall-mounted offices.

The main thrust of the Met's share of the New Works Programme was to improve capacity between London and Harrow where house-building was now proceeding at a tremendous rate, each new home bringing with it at least one new passenger on a railway already under some considerable pressure. The pinch-point was at Finchley Road where four tracks converged into two by means of a flat junction just south of the station. Duplication of the old brick tunnels was regarded as impractical, which implied a new route would need to be chosen. It was not that the Met had ignored the problem. In 1925 it had examined a scheme for building a tube line from Kilburn to Edgware Road station, running beneath that road itself, and promising some relief for the Finchley Road tunnels. The line was planned to leave the existing route north of Kilburn and drop down steeply into twin tube tunnels sufficiently large to accommodate the full sized rolling stock. At Edgware Road station the line would rise to join the Inner Circle just west of the platforms (though unhelpfully by means of a flat junction), and the station would be rebuilt. Three intermediate stations were envisaged at Quex Road, Kilburn Park Road and Clifton Road. For several reasons nothing was done, apart from the rebuilding of Edgware Road station with four platforms with provision in the signalling for the new line when built. In a desperate attempt to ease the congestion, Marlborough Road and St John's Wood stations were closed during the morning rush hour from 1929. While this helped the train service to a limited extent it did nothing for local passengers who were deprived of a station at the very time they most wanted to use it.

In 1930 a further tube scheme was considered, this time running beneath the existing line to Baker Street, then rising to join the Inner Circle to the west of Great Portland Street station. This very expensive full-sized tube suggestion was also felt unjustified and a much simpler proposal was examined to replace the Finchley Road flat junction with a flying junction formed by a short tube line carrying the northbound fast trains beneath the slow lines just north of Swiss Cottage. This, too, was not proceeded with, and the Met's attention began to be seriously diverted by considerations of its own impending oblivion.

The LPTB were able to take a wider view than that taken by the Met, and realised that to the south of Baker Street there existed the Bakerloo Line which was operating at less than its full potential capacity. This opened up the possibility of projecting 'Metropolitan' trains through to the West End if the lines could be linked. A possible solution was therefore to build a link between Finchley Road and Baker Street (Bakerloo), thereby (in effect) duplicating the Finchley Road tunnels and opening up more journey possibilities than hitherto. It also avoided overloading the Inner Circle with more trains or taxing further the restricted terminal facilities of Baker Street (Met). A key factor now was that trains proceeding onto the Bakerloo Line would have to be of the smaller 'tube' stock type which was not suitable for long journeys. This implied that it was better to transfer the local services onto the Bakerloo, which mainly originated from Stanmore or intermediately. Journey opportunities could be much increased by providing good interchange at Wembley Park so that people from the Stanmore branch could change onto faster trains to the City, and at Finchley Road where passengers from stations to Neasden could do the same. This would mean rearranging the tracks so that the local lines ran between the fast ones, enabling cross-platform interchange to be offered at Wembley Park and Finchley Road.

Parliamentary powers were obtained in 1935 for a new line to run more or less beneath the existing Metropolitan Line, linking into the existing station at Swiss Cottage, which was to be retained. A new station was to be built in the St John's Wood area called Acacia Road, about mid-way between the existing St John's Wood and Marlborough Road stations both of which were to be closed (though it was initially desired that the original St John's Wood would be opened for important cricket matches at Lords, which name it assumed from June 1939). At Baker Street the new link met the Bakerloo just east of the existing station on the southbound line, and just to the west on the northbound line; this arrangement required an additional southbound platform and meant trains converging at the junction could wait in platform areas.

Work began in April 1936 and was pushed ahead quickly. At Baker Street both the old and the new southbound platforms straddled a new lower concourse area from which a pair of escalators rose up to meet an enlargement of the existing interchange concourse under the Metropolitan Line, to which it was linked by short stairways. A further pair of new escalators conveyed Bakerloo Line passengers to a new ticket hall area at street level, situated at the corner of upper Baker Street and Marylebone Road. This was connected to the existing Metropolitan Line ticket hall (next door but at a lower level) by stairs. At Finchley Road a second island platform was needed to service what were to be the new southbound tracks – the existing island was retained in a modified form for northbound services. At West Hampstead the island was in the wrong place and the only solution was to build a new one displaced sideways a few feet farther north-east, requiring some bridge alterations. Kilburn was fairly easy as the existing southbound platform could be adapted to form an island, with the old northbound platform abandoned. Dollis Hill, like West Hampstead, required bodily movement of the platform. Very little work was required to the stations at Willesden Green, Neasden or Wembley Park, where platforms already existed on all tracks. All stations between Finchley Road and Stanmore had platform heights adjusted to 'compromise' height to suit both Metropolitan Line and tube stock trains (except for platforms on the 'fast' lines).

Most of the stations on this section were improved in some way. At Finchley Road and West Hampstead the existing station buildings were retained while the interiors were entirely refurbished to the latest standards. At platform level new buildings were erected with integral canopy, and at West Hampstead flower beds were installed. At Kilburn the existing entrance and ticket hall were completely rebuilt and refurbished, although the former southbound stairs were retained in their original form; at platform level completely new structures were provided. Both Willesden Green and Neasden survived substantially unmolested. Dollis Hill received a modernised ticket hall, with necessary other adjustments to suit the resited platform above; again completely new platform facilities were provided. Wembley Park received some adjustments, but again remained largely unmodified. No changes were needed on the Stanmore branch other than platform height adjustments.

Track rearrangement was tied into replacement of all the signalling, which although modified was still basically that installed in 1914. One of the earliest works to be completed was a new signal box at Finchley Road, commissioned on 25th July 1937. This was equipped with a 59-lever frame incorporating 'push-pull' route levers, which also controlled West Hampstead. Other new signal boxes (all with conventional single function levers) were brought into use at Stanmore (47 levers) on 29th May 1938, Neasden South (93 levers) on 27th June 1938, Willesden Green (59 levers) on 11th September 1938, and Neasden North (47 levers) on 22nd May 1939. The existing electrically interlocked cabin at Wembley Park was retained, although the signal frame was re-locked to suit the new layout. At Stanmore the signalling and pointwork was all-electric as it was not felt worthwhile to provide an air main – and so ended the very short life of the innovative CTC system. All the existing electro-mechanical signal boxes were closed during this period, and the intermediate electro-pneumatic semaphores were all replaced by coloured light signals worked by a.c. track circuits.

Rearrangement of the tracks required very detailed planning. The biggest operation took place over the weekend of 17th/18th September 1938 when the tracks between Finchley Road and Dollis Hill were re-organised into the form in which they are today. In essence the direction of running of the two inner tracks was reversed and they became the two new 'local' lines. The outer pair of tracks (formerly northbound local and southbound fast lines) became the new 'fast' lines, but retained their existing direction of running. The work also involved major changes to the platform arrangements at West Hampstead, Kilburn and Dollis Hill. All was ready for traffic on Monday morning, though creditably it had been possible to operate a limited service on the Sunday too, all the more remarkable when it is considered that all the signalling was replaced at the same time, with new two-aspect coloured light signals, and with new track, points and sidings brought into use. During this phase the new island platform at

Finchley Road was commissioned between what were now to be the southbound tracks. South of the station the southbound line was diverted on to a new alignment for nearly a quarter of a mile, necessitated by the need to leave sufficient room for the future Bakerloo tunnels to surface. A temporary connection was made just south of the station to allow trains from what is now the southbound local line to join the new alignment; similarly on the northbound line a junction (this time permanent) just south of the station gave access to the new northbound local platform.

North of Dollis Hill the existing direction of running was unchanged, requiring a junction just north of the station where the two local lines crossed on the flat to resume their original direction of running. To control this critical junction a temporary 7-lever signalbox was provided at Dollis Hill. To reduce the pressure on this flat junction some southbound local trains from Wembley went along the fast lines until a point south of Neasden where a temporary crossover allowed them to resume the correct line before reaching Dollis Hill. From Monday 7th November 1938 the revised direction of running was extended northwards to Preston Road and the temporary crossover and signal box near Dollis Hill were removed. Track re-arrangement at Wembley Park included the replacement of the Stanmore Line junction with a new flyover. Again a limited service was maintained on the intervening Sunday.

With Acton Works assuming responsibility for heavy overhaul of Met stock, the transfer of most of the steam and goods fleet to the LNER, and the arrival of 'new technology' underground trains on the Met and Bakerloo Lines, the facilities provided at Neasden Works were now unsuitable and outdated. Furthermore the arrangements at the existing Bakerloo depots at London Road and Queen's Park were quite inadequate and Neasden would have to provide the major facility for the whole Bakerloo Line as well at the Met. London Transport soon took the decision to demolish the whole of the existing works and build new depot and stabling facilities on the site to the latest standards, based on recent experience at Cockfosters and Northfields. Work began on demolition of the existing depot in 1936 but was inevitably slow because while all the work was in hand it was still home to a sizeable fleet of trains (some quite old) that still required maintenance. What emerged were 14 under-cover roads for maintenance, several of which were double length, including a 3-road lifting shop, and a 4-road cleaning shed. Twenty-three open-air sidings were provided, mainly double length, and at the north end of the depot was a 2-road shed for the remaining steam locomotives. Work was completed in 1939.

It was not until 2nd November 1939 that Bakerloo trains began operating between Stanmore and Elephant & Castle. Under the new arrangements services between Wembley Park and Stanmore were entirely handed over to Bakerloo Line trains, as were most of the local services between Wembley Park and Finchley Road. In the peaks six Met trains per hour (all from Rayners Lane) called all-stations between Wembley Park and Finchley Road, and these and certain other Met trains also called at Swiss Cottage; these did not continue beyond August 1940 when the Met ticket hall and platforms at Swiss Cottage were closed and all local trains between Wembley Park and Baker Street became Bakerloo. A number of trains terminated short at Wembley Park and Willesden Green. 'Lords' and Marlborough Road stations were closed and the earlier plans to re-open the former station during cricket matches foundered because of the Second World War.

The New Works Programme also addressed the Met&GC section north of Harrow where the two tracks were now struggling to carry the mix of all-stations, semi-fast and main line trains and where there was considerable traffic development potential. The

This 1936 south-looking view of Harrow-on-the-Hill shows the local platforms (added in 1908) incorporating Smith's bookstall and window displays for local shops, including Soper's store. The platforms (two side and an island) were connected by subway, the only part of the station to survive the comprehensive reconstruction not completed until 1948. The platform in view is now incorporated in present day platform 5. LT Museum

answer was to install a second pair of tracks as far as Rickmansworth, which was then considered to be the outer edge of the main suburban belt. Initial plans even considered duplicating platforms on the new tracks at every station (it must be remembered that certain express trains served some of these stations). Electrification north of Rickmansworth was to have been less comprehensive, although passing loops were intended at Chorleywood.

The changes south of Wembley Park ordained that the tracks as far as Harrow would also need to be arranged so that the 'slow' lines ran between the fast. As mentioned previously this arrangement came into use to a point north of Preston Road from 3rd October 1938, requiring a new southbound fast track to be built on the eastern side of the (comparatively new) island platform, vacating the space previously taken alongside the northbound fast. This, temporary, arrangement required the southbound fast to cross the two local lines on the level a few hundred yards north of the station, a temporary signal box being provided to control movements.

The plan at Harrow-on-the-Hill was to build additional platform faces at the back of the existing southbound local and northbound through platforms, increasing the number of faces from four to six, thereby matching the number of platforms with the number of approach tracks in each direction. This meant demolishing the existing platform buildings and the construction of new station facilities on an overbridge. On the south side a vast parcels sorting depot was built linked by parcels lift to the subway running under the platforms (platforms 1–4 were also linked to the subway by parcels lifts). North of Harrow two additional roads were to be laid, mainly on the western side, as far as Rickmansworth, for which some land had already been acquired. Work proceeded until the Second World War forced progress to stop, leaving Harrow-on-the-Hill a partial building site and the very awkward crossover at Preston Road restraining further growth in passenger capacity.

North of Rickmansworth it was intended to extend the electrified area out as far as Amersham and Chesham, which together with the abandonment of locomotive changes at Rickmansworth was expected to save eight minutes on the journey to Baker Street. Chesham branch working had always been an operational irritation as locos had to run round their trains at each terminus. In 1936 an AEC diesel railcar was tested on the line following which an order was placed for two cars, though this was soon cancelled because of price increases and the option to electrify. Now it was proposed to run more through trains on the Chesham branch by splitting trains at Chalfont & Latimer (as Chalfont Road had become in November 1915). Electrification beyond Amersham was also desirable but was not considered worthwhile in view of the limited electric services possible and the long distances involved. Regrettably the war meant nothing was done.

In early London Transport days the steam stock trains were operating in 5- or 6-carriage formations but the majority of the electric stock was operating as trains of seven or eight coaches, at least during the rush hours. In the interests of efficiency major overhaul was transferred from Neasden to the former Underground central overhaul works at Acton where various modifications ensued. At first LT was disinclined to change the overall service pattern but busied itself in reducing the varying types of incompatible rolling stock in use on the Met. An early outcome was the standardisation of the majority of 1927–31 coaches into a fully compatible fleet of 'MW' formations, producing seventeen 8-coach trains. Some 26 remaining motor coaches remained available as part of a pool to haul older stock.

The 1936 timetable is illustrative of what was on offer. Between 8am and 9am at Baker Street (southbound) there were 31 trains, of which 15 worked through to the City. Of all these trains six came from Stanmore (with another two Stanmore shuttles connecting with other trains) and these all terminated at Baker Street; five trains came from Watford, eight from Uxbridge, three from Rayners Lane, one from Aylesbury, two from Rickmansworth, four from Wembley Park and two from Harrow. This was supplemented during the same period with two Marylebone trains from Aylesbury and one from Rickmansworth. The Stanmores, Wembleys and Harrows served the local stations south of Wembley, excepting Marlborough Road and St John's Wood which were then closed in the morning rush hour. Most trains stopped at most stations between Wembley Park and their points of origin, though some missed out Wembley Park and either Northwick Park or Preston Road, a few missed out Northwood and Northwood Hills, and the 8.25 from Uxbridge ran fast from Ruislip (but did call at Harrow and Northwick Park). The Aylesbury train ran fast from Northwood to Baker Street. Fastest times to Baker Street were: 1 hour 13 minutes from Aylesbury, 43 minutes from Amersham, 36 minutes from Watford and 34 minutes from Uxbridge.

The arrival of the Bakerloo Line in 1939 of itself made little impact on Met services, except that all trains now stopped at Finchley Road, and a few of the erstwhile 'Stanmore' paths between Finchley Road and Baker Street were available to improve other services. However, there were other major changes in the wind. London Transport had watched with mounting concern the steadily increasing traffic at the east end of the District Line, particularly between Whitechapel and Barking. An obvious solution was to switch or extend trains from the north side of the Inner Circle that terminated at Aldgate or Whitechapel or ran through to the East London Line. Initially a proportion of Hammersmith & City Line trains were switched to Barking from the East London Line and nine additional 6-car trains (known as the M and N classes) were ordered to existing District Line designs as this could be done quickly.

London Transport soon projected Piccadilly Line trains to Uxbridge and the contrast between the two types of rolling stock is significant. The Metropolitan train, alongside the 'downside' platform is composed of former steam-hauled 'bogie' stock converted to electric multiple unit control. The station was soon to be superseded by a new one in the High Street.

However, because of a number of short platforms, the Hammersmith & City trains were restricted in length to no more than six coaches so a better option appeared to be to extend to Barking some of the 8-coach trains hitherto reversing at Aldgate, those originating from the Uxbridge line being selected for reasons discussed shortly. This move inevitably meant the further intermingling of services operating on the sub-surface railways, much expanding the possibilities of delays on one service impacting on all the others, a problem never easily soluble where frequency-dependent services intermixed with those operating to a published timetable. (It is worth recalling that the Met was hitherto renowned for its punctuality – a former Metropolitan Railway director recalled that in its heyday any delay of more than two minutes was given unwelcome exposure at board meetings).

London Transport announced its arrival at Ickenham with a prominent new sign, but a new station had to wait until 1971. When opened in 1905 the station didn't even have the booking hut, visible here. Dennis Edwards collection

London Transport recognised that much of the rolling stock it had inherited from the Metropolitan Railway was quite old and would need imminent replacement. LT wanted to develop a new type of train, in many ways very much from the former Underground Group stable but technically quite radical. Perhaps inevitably it took some while to get the new design into production, which required other measures to be taken in the interim. The first was to replace the antiquated stock on the Hammersmith & City Line, which dated back to 1905. The replacement trains were sleek, flair sided saloon cars designated the O Stock and operated in semi-permanently coupled 2-car units which could be made up into 4-car and 6-car trains using fully automatic couplers at their outer ends. Note that from this point new vehicles are referred to as 'cars' following former Underground Group practice. Each unit (of which there were to be 58) was to be controlled by a single electrical equipment called a metadyne, which was a rotating machine which converted the constant voltage input into the constant current required by the motors; this 'stepless' control allowed higher rates of acceleration to be used and could be operated in reverse to provide regeneration of current during braking. The design entered service in 1937.

For the Met main services it was proposed to introduce trains of a broadly similar type, but adapted for operation in 8-car formations, and this was to be called the P Stock. These trains needed to replace a broadly similar number of the oldest Met coaches but would be totally incompatible with them in nearly every way. In consequence it was thought desirable to separate them so far as possible by restricting their use to one single service group, that to Uxbridge being selected because of its overall characteristics of denser service and comparatively short station distances.

The P Stock was intended to operate in mainly 8-car formations consisting of a pair of 3-car units and one 2-car unit. The 3-car units were to include a trailer car which would have a body identical to the motor cars to the extent of including driving cab doors, though they were sealed and the cab space was fitted with seats; this was intended to facilitate their future conversion to motor cars, a vague long term objective. As the Met Line still accommodated first class passengers it was arranged that the trailers would be divided into two saloon areas separated by a communicating door. One of the resulting sections was to devoted to first class passengers and had a different type of seat covering – about the only distinction possible in such a carriage. The main doors were to be air-operated under the overriding control of the guard but with local passenger open buttons to reduce unnecessary door operations, especially at open-air stations in cold weather. Complications arose in that for various reasons some nineteen 2-car units of O Stock were almost immediately surplus to requirements. However they could not easily be used on the Met main line because the guard's controls were in the driving cabs whereas those on the P Stock were in the passenger saloons. In consequence these units were split up and the cars distributed amongst the P Stock trains in positions where the guard's controls would not normally be required.

From 17th July 1939 through services were introduced between Uxbridge and Barking, the entire Uxbridge service running through at about 7–8 minute intervals. As P Stock did not begin to enter service until that date the M/N trains, together with others intended for the District line, had to hold the fort. The Uxbridge–Barking service was seriously interrupted by damage in central London during the blitz, and after through services settled down, the daunting operational practicalities became evident. It was withdrawn with effect from 6th October 1941 (with through Hammersmith & City–Barking trains resuming) and Uxbridge services reverted to Aldgate during the rush hours and Baker Street off-peak.

Delivery of the new trains implied disposal of the old ones. Amongst those to go were most of the pre-1913 electric stock including the bogie stock converted for electric use. Six of these carriages survived, however. To improve efficiency of the Chesham shuttle while electrification was on hold, it was desired to introduce 'push-pull' working where the loco did not run round the train at each end of the journey; it followed that in one direction the locomotive would be at the rear. To deal with this method of operation special controls had to be fitted in the leading carriage which would remotely drive the locomotive. Two dedicated 3-carriage trains were required – one always a standby for the other – and six 'bogie' stock coaches were selected, two being of 1898 origin. In their converted form they took over the shuttle in 1941 and lasted another 20 years: not a bad life to get from them.

As a further impact of wartime conditions first-class accommodation was abolished on local Met trains and those to the Uxbridge line from the 1st February 1940 and from 6th October 1941 on trains to the Met&GC section (this included all LNER trains from Marylebone except for certain through trains beyond Aylesbury).

This view of a P Stock train at Rayners Lane also shows the back of the new station building and updated platforms – all three features demonstrating the new designs that swept in as part of London Transport's 1935-40 New Works Programme. LT Museum

The Second World War caused the introduction of blackout conditions at stations and in trains (which were soon fitted with dim reading lights) and various other measures to deal with the exigency. However the Met spread so much beyond the central London built up area, and was so little in tunnel, that it was in many senses much less badly affected by wartime events than many other lines. The obvious exception to this generalisation was the operation over the north side of the Circle Line to Aldgate, which was constantly affected by bombing, especially east of King's Cross where large areas of the City were absolutely devastated and train services were sometimes interrupted for weeks on end. North of Baker Street bombing occasionally caused delays or damage, but to a much smaller extent. Finchley Road, Willesden Green and Wembley Park were all damaged by bombs, though not seriously. Stanmore Junction was hit twice and several bombs landed on Neasden depot but caused little damage.

Wartime bomb damage affected the City sections very much more than the open-air Metropolitan. However, Baker Street was hit and this view shows serious damage to the southern wing of the General Office building. Mild interest may be noted from passengers in the train at platform 4 below (the train windows are open to let light in as netting was pasted over the glass). LT Museum

By far the most serious occurrence was the demolition of a 70ft length of viaduct near Kilburn, but what is perhaps surprising in all the circumstances is the speed at which services were got moving again. At 2.46am on the morning of 15th September 1940 a high explosive bomb hit the northbound viaduct just south of Kilburn station completely demolishing three arches and producing a large crater in the ground over which was heaped an enormous pile of rubble. The immediate response was a fleet of buses to ferry passengers across the gap, with trains shuttling to stations either side. By 10am decisions about service restoration had already been taken. The services were all to be run over the little-damaged southbound viaduct with the southbound local (Bakerloo) line resignalled for northbound trains and all southbound trains (Met and Bakerloo) worked over the southbound fast line. The northbound line north of West Hampstead was slewed across to meet the southbound local line so northbound trains could gain access; an existing crossover at Dollis Hill was used to restore right line running. The total distance of track resignalled exceeded two miles and also required power cables to be shifted to allow the track connection to be installed. Astonishingly the work was completed by 6pm the following day notwithstanding that it had to stop during the previous night because of the blackout, and that workers were harassed by an enemy aircraft.

The next task was to clear away the debris and reconstruct the northbound viaduct on a temporary basis. Debris amounted to about 1500 tons and the ground was so badly affected that even for the restoration of temporary supports it was necessary to put in new foundations 12 feet below the surface. Three timber lattice piers were built with wooden struts between to keep the affair rigid. Pairs of steel joists were fixed across the top (two under each running rail) tied together with timber baulks. New sleepered trackwork was laid directly on top of the steelwork and attached with long bolts. The whole affair weighed 85 tons. In this safe but inelegant-looking fashion it was possible to restore normal 4-track operation within 14 days, the brickwork being subsequently rebuilt with minimal interruption to traffic. In the meantime the track-slew was replaced by an emergency crossover to facilitate engineers' train operation, though it was subsequently removed.

During the war the northern end of the Met&GC served significant military and construction establishments, notably International Alloys at Aylesbury (valuable to the Ministry of Aircraft Production) and a military establishment at Quainton Road, where in both cases new sidings were installed. In May 1943 it proved necessary to augment passenger services between Aylesbury and Quainton Road in the early evening, and this was achieved by projecting one Met train that previously reversed at Aylesbury, and back-projecting one LNER train which previously started at Aylesbury. At first these extensions were unadvertised to the general public, but from 7th January 1946 they became normal advertised trains. The emergency over, they were cut back to Aylesbury from 31st May 1948, and the Met never again served Quainton Road. Another valuable facility was the RAF camp at Halton, near Wendover, which had been connected to the Met&GC by a 1-mile private railway since the previous emergency in 1918 (the connection was only removed in 1963).

The war also reduced the Met's electric locos to workshop grey livery as the need for repainting arose. Nameplates also disappeared slowly, ostensibly in the scrap drive, though the last was only removed in 1948 so its contribution to the war effort must have been limited! Fifteen surviving locomotives received new aluminium alloy nameplates in the early 1950s as Met sentimentality remained strong.

Wartime took its toll on the general level of maintenance and left the Met in a much run-down condition falling far short of the ideals that had been aspired to beforehand. It was to be a further 15 years before any of this could really be put right.

The electric locomotive (still in its wartime livery) has just backed onto its train at Rickmansworth, the steam locomotive having come off. Don Jones

A new post war era

From 1st January 1948 much of Britain's inland transport was nationalised, the component parts becoming vested in the British Transport Commission (BTC). The BTC itself retained ownership of property but was required to distribute responsibility for operation of the various different classes of service to statutory 'executives'. The main line railways went to the Railway Executive and the former LPTB operations to the London Transport Executive (LTE). The BTC was not in the business of setting up joint committees to run things so the operation of the now-abolished Met&GC (and Met&LNE) joint committees had to be merged into one body or another. The usual basis for allocation of assets was to give them to the predominant user, and the decision was made to transfer the line between Harrow South Junction and Aylesbury South Junction to the LTE, and Aylesbury station and points north to the Railway Executive (this was achieved formally from 25th June 1950). There was a degree of logic to this in that Aylesbury also served the Wycombe branch, the main ex-Great Central trains called there, and the staffing and operations had always been separate from the Met&GC operation. North of Aylesbury LT trains no longer ran. South of Aylesbury, the electrified (or shortly to be electrified) operations more naturally sat with LT, notwithstanding a significant 'main line' presence (goods, parcels and stopping main line trains). Furthermore, stations south of Aylesbury were already staffed by LT. However, following the practice adopted at the beginning of 1933, rulebooks continued to be split at Rickmansworth, still the actual limit of electrification, with main line rules applying to the north. Aylesbury, incidentally, quickly became Aylesbury Town to avoid confusion with Aylesbury LMS station (relocated in 1888), which became Aylesbury High Street. The lines south of Harrow that were leased by the Met to the LNER were transferred to the Railway Executive.

Reorganisation took time. As a preliminary, from 17th June 1950 track maintenance between Aylesbury South and the old Met&GC maintenance boundary at milepost 28½ was transferred from the Railway Executive to London Transport. It took a little longer for satisfactory arrangements to be made to hand over signalling maintenance to LT, which followed on 7th October.

Taking over most of the joint line required LT to engage in a wide range of quite alien administrative arrangements, including renewed familiarity with parcels traffic and booking goods and loading goods wagons. There was also the continuing operation of main-line style ticket booking arrangements; it was still possible to book a ticket to any station in the country, including accompanying merchandise (from parcels to horses) and there was a daunting variety of tickets which had to be kept available: the fares north of Harrow continued on the main line scale until the 1970s, though the variety of tickets reduced drastically from around 1966. There was still a sizeable number of 'protected' joint staff, who could not be used elsewhere.

The responsibility for goods and parcels was soon given over to the Railway Executive, and from 2nd June 1950 the London Midland Region formally took control of these activities from the Eastern Region (it was always regarded as LMR goods territory); in practice the LT staff on site were compelled to remain responsible for the actual handling at stations (as agents of the LMR), retaining thereby the dual responsibility they had had in joint line days, though LT management was able to avoid direct contact with all this troublesome traffic.

There was also the agonising question as to which of the Railway Executive's regions the rest of the ex-GC main line should be placed, not an easy question given its geography on the one hand and the bureaucratic desire for discrete regional areas on the other. Upon nationalisation the existing organisational status quo was necessarily retained notwithstanding the abolition of the Joint Committee. The Eastern Region thus stepped into the shoes of the LNER. From 2nd April 1950 the lines between Marylebone and Harrow were transferred to the Western Region, while those north of Aylesbury South Junction went to the London Midland Region. Both the passenger and goods trains and their motive power were necessarily supplied by the Eastern Region, which reflected the practical needs of the ex-GC line as a whole.

These very complicated arrangements (involving three British Railways regions) were changed again in 1958 when the ex-GC line from Marylebone to beyond Quainton Road (except for the LT section between Harrow and Aylesbury South) was transferred to the LMR for all purposes. This resulted for the first time in the general introduction of LMR motive power, which including the locomotives hauling the Met trains. A variety of ex-LNER locomotives had previously been used on Met trains by the Eastern Region, latterly mainly L1 2-6-4 tanks (the Chesham shuttle usually used C13 4-4-2 tanks). The LMR employed a variety of its own 2-6-4 tanks, including a few of the BR standard design (except on the Chesham shuttle where 2-6-2 tanks were used). It was under LMR control that Aylesbury Town reverted to Aylesbury upon closure of the competing station in 1962.

During 1948 Wembley Park station had been considerably expanded in preparation for the 1948 Olympic Games, focused on Wembley stadium. The old station building remained largely unaltered from Metropolitan Railway days, but to handle Olympic traffic a new station structure was built alongside, connected by a wide gallery to new stairways half-way along each platform. Although the Olympic ticket hall was never used for everyday traffic, it remained an essential part of the station's ability to cater for the crowds travelling to the Wembley complex for major events.

With war out of the way thoughts turned, very slowly, to the need to complete the 4-tracking work abandoned in 1940. Most pressing was the completion of the new track layout at Harrow-on-the-Hill which would abolish the awkward 'temporary' flat junction north of Preston Road, offer two more platform faces at Harrow and introduce modern signalling controlled from one new power signal box (all of which would enable four signal boxes to be closed). This work was regarded as urgent and it restarted in 1946. The first significant part of the commissioning took place on 28th February 1948 when the local roads south of Harrow were shifted onto their new alignment. From 7th March the flat crossing at Preston Road was removed and the tracks rearranged such that to Harrow South Junction the local lines ran between the fast (and at Northwick Park a new southbound fast line was commissioned on the north side). From 18th April 1948 the new signalling was commissioned at Harrow North Junction with track rearrangement so that the southbound Met and Eastern Region lines were split at Harrow North, the Metropolitan Line now running to the east rather than the west of the Uxbridge covered way (requiring rearrangement of the goods yard). From 2nd May the commissioning was completed. This final stage required replacement of Harrow Station and Harrow South Junction signalling and the commissioning of two additional platform roads (present platforms 1 and 6). Henceforth platform 1 was intended for use by northbound Eastern Region and non-stop Metropolitan Line trains to Aylesbury and Uxbridge, platform 2 for London-bound Eastern Region trains, 3 and 4 for northbound Met trains (generally 3 for Watford line and 4 for Uxbridge) and 5 and 6 for southbound Metropolitan Line trains.

The signalling was unique. From the vantage point of the new station signal box, mounted high on the station overbridge, the signalman commanded a 97-lever signal frame divided into two portions. The left hand end of 40 levers was equipped with push-pull route levers, the operation of which set complete routes. The right-hand end of 47 levers contained the usual full stroke signal and point levers for operating equipment just north of Harrow station, but most of these were operated automatically by compressed air motors in accordance with the route levers controlled by the signalman. Similarly the signal boxes at Harrow North (35 levers) and Harrow South (23 levers) were normally unmanned and the levers were controlled remotely from the master frame at Harrow station. The system (which is still in use) had the advantages of reducing the cabling required, speeding up operation, and allowing the signalman to pre-select routes which would be set up when conflicting trains had got out of the way. The automatic levers were controlled by small compressed air motors and if in an emergency the air was switched off then the frames could be operated manually. The panoramic vantage point was also helpful, though, as if to demonstrate just how high it was, it was struck by lightning just before commissioning as no lightning conductor had then been fitted. Another unusual feature of the Harrow layout was the use of moveable angles on four of the crossings used at higher speeds than usual – these were not and are not liked by LT because they are a maintenance liability notwithstanding the better ride they offer trains.

It is perhaps of little surprise that the untidy track arrangements at Wembley Park were to prove an operational nightmare. Apart from the complicated platform working, the main problem was that what had by now grown to six tracks at Wembley Park station converged into four tracks for the half-mile to the junction where the Stanmore line peeled off. This meant Metropolitan Line 'slow' trains had to manoeuvre their way between either the Met 'fast' trains or the Bakerloo Line trains before regaining their own tracks. The answer was to construct an additional pair of tracks between Wembley Park and Stanmore Junction on the northern side, requiring further reduction of the carriage shed to five roads. The opportunity was also taken to simplify considerably the track layout at Wembley Park station itself. The works were taken in hand in 1953 and the new southbound track commissioned on 27th June 1954, at which time a temporary 59-lever signal box was commissioned. The new northbound line was brought into use on 26th September 1954, segregating entirely the Met and Bakerloo services apart from a few empty stock movements. At the same time a push-button control desk was commissioned in the old signal box, operating by electro-pneumatic means part of the former signal frame that had been retained to provide the mechanical interlocking component (the electric locking being superseded).

The scheme for modernisation of the former joint line had to wait until money was available, though as a preliminary a new signal box was built at Rickmansworth on 6th December 1953. This was built at the northern end of the station and was of standard LT design with a conventional 47-lever frame; the mechanical box at the south end of the station was decommissioned and subsequently removed. By this time it had already been decided that the pre-war intention to extend 4-track operation into Rickmansworth itself was unnecessary, so the existing trackwork and loco-changing facilities went unaltered. The installation deviated slightly from the LT standard in that 3 and 4-aspect signals were used for some of the running signals, notwithstanding the 25 mph speed restriction throughout the whole area. A year later (from 5th December) the signals at Chorleywood were converted from semaphore to track-circuit operated coloured light. This time the existing signal frame was retained because it only needed to be used during shunting; normally the signals operated automatically. Thenceforth track circuit operated coloured light signalling was in use throughout the Metropolitan Line to a point between Chorleywood and Chalfont & Latimer. By this time thoughts of passing loops at Chorleywood had been dropped.

Limited physical track works had in fact started north of Moor Park in 1950 as part of a scheme to replace three adjacent overbridges. Much of the 4-track formation had already been constructed here and it was decided that the simplest means of renewing the bridges would be to slew the two tracks onto the new formation upon which the replacement bridges could be erected without interfering with the traffic. From 4th June 1950 about 2500 feet of track was shifted onto the new alignment, which included Watford South Junction itself, which had to be completely realigned.

Another improvement which took place in this area was the abolition of the old Watford Junction signal box (of 28 mechanical levers) and its replacement by a remote controlled 'interlocking machine' operated by a push button panel in Rickmansworth signal box. An interlocking machine was in effect a lever frame with mechanical interlocking which was specifically designed for remote operation, the vertically-mounted levers being moved (as at Harrow) by small air motors; they could in emergency be hand-operated by trained signal department staff. The new panel at Rickmansworth contained 16 push buttons controlling 12 signals and seven sets of points at all three junctions; the existing illuminated track diagram was extended to cover the increased area. The new signalling came into use on 25th September 1955.

This 1950s view of the Chesham shuttle train at Chesham shows off well the Victorian carriages and a station little altered since opening. P.H. Groom

The remainder of the 4-tracking scheme had to wait its turn, and authority to proceed was eventually granted during 1956. It was perhaps unsurprisingly less complex than that envisaged pre-war. Continuing the earlier theme two additional tracks would be built, mainly on the western side of the existing tracks, between Harrow North Junction and a point just north of Watford South Junction; these would become what were termed the 'main' lines, the existing tracks becoming the 'local' lines. No additional platforms would be built on the main lines except at Pinner and, perversely, Moor Park (the least heavily used station) where it was felt helpful to allow for interchange for local traffic between the Rickmansworth and Watford branches (the direct train service having been abandoned by LT from January 1934). This round-the-corner journey was always far more difficult than using the good bus service between those towns, but a few preferred the rail route and some were even content to pay the premium fare imposed by LT for the privilege of being taken two miles out of their way via Moor Park! Four tracking into a rebuilt Rickmansworth station was no longer on the cards, and it would only be possible for Watford trains to gain access to the local tracks. Planning continued during 1957, by which time plans for 'fast' platforms at Pinner had been abandoned, and site works began towards the back end of 1958.

The work consisted of two key elements. The first was extension of electrification to Amersham and Chesham, its completion around 1960 allowing interim service improvements to take place. There was then the 4-tracking which would permit service acceleration and an increase in frequency. When complete, the services north of Amersham would be provided exclusively by British Railways, itself introducing diesel multiple unit trains on the local services. A temporary depot was established in the under-utilised goods yard at Willesden Green, where rail welding and the manufacturing of concrete cable posts took place.

During 1959 works progressed rapidly north of Rickmansworth where new substations at Chalfont & Latimer and Chorleywood, and a signal box at Amersham, had been built and were being equipped. From 25th October 1959 new track circuit controlled coloured light signalling was introduced at Chalfont & Latimer; this was operated from a local interlocking machine temporarily controlled from a panel in the old signal box. South of Rickmansworth work began on the 4-tracking in the autumn of 1959 and the re-equipping of the substation at Croxleyhall was in hand.

From 20th March 1960 the new signal box at Amersham was commissioned, together with coloured light signals and track circuits on what was largely the existing track layout. The new signal box, to the south of the station, was in a fresh style but retained the operating floor at first storey level. The signals and points were controlled by an interlocking machine in the ground floor relay room. At first floor level the signalman was provided with a push button control desk and illuminated diagram similar to that at Wembley Park. Provision was made on the control panel for operating at a later stage the signals at Chalfont and Latimer.

The physical works at Amersham were curiously substantial considering the improved train service then contemplated. Two reversing sidings were provided north of the station, and a third platform was added mainly for northbound Aylesbury trains; both of the northbound platforms could also be used for reversing trains north to south. In addition a northbound goods loop was built so that passenger trains could overtake slower freight traffic. The new platform was built at the back of the existing 'down' platform, converting it into an island and requiring substantial adjustment to the platform buildings. The new platform, goods loop and one siding were commissioned from 22nd May 1960 from when passenger trains could more conveniently be turned

Chesham on the first day of electric operation with a 'through' train in the old platform and the steam-hauled shuttle in the new but short-lived bay. LT Museum

at Amersham. From the same date control of the signalling at Chalfont was transferred to Amersham signal box. The second siding and final signalling and trackwork were completed on 19th June.

Chesham also benefited. The electric 'tablet' working, by which the single line had been safely operated for many years, had been replaced in 1949 by single line working controlled by track circuit. This was not suitable for the new order and it was now believed useful when a through train was on the line to allow the shuttle train to lay over at Chesham as well as at Chalfont. This required the conversion of Chesham's former prize-winning flowerbed into a new bay platform, long enough to hide away the shuttle train while the through train was on the move. Some changes took effect from 12th June 1960 when the approach signals were altered from mechanical to coloured light. The new platform was commissioned on 3rd July and included trap points so that all could be quite sure the shuttle could not unwittingly escape. The elderly signal box at Chesham was retained and modified for the new arrangements but some mechanical signals remained.

The new signalling and trackwork hardly came into their own until it was possible for electric trains to reach Amersham, achieved on Sunday 14th August 1960 when the electrification works had been completed. After some route training the new timetable from 12th September 1960 saw the Chesham shuttle now operating electrically. There were virtually no other changes except for occasional off peak all-stations Amersham trains robbed from the Watford service, and other odd journeys including a through Chesham train hauled throughout by an electric locomotive. Chesham's first weekday passenger train of the day had for many years been operated by steam-hauled main line stock bound for Marylebone; this continued after electrification, though now diesel hauled, and was not replaced until 18th June 1962 by a through Baker Street electric working. The Aylesbury service carried on unaltered for the time being with locos continuing to be exchanged at Rickmansworth.

T Stock train approaching Moor Park in 1958. The platform ends (just visible) are at approximately the point where tracks have been severed in the photo below.

At Moor Park the old wooden station was swept away and an entirely new 4-track station built. In this north-looking view the service has been switched to the new tracks and platforms on the left (the future fast lines) while the old station was demolished to allow the future slow line platforms to be built. LT Museum

Commissioning the new 4-track works took place entirely during 1961 and 1962. The first stage took place on 5th February 1961 when the new 'main' tracks were introduced between Northwood Hills and Northwood on the west side of the old lines. Just north of Northwood Hills access was gained to the new lines by means of a double junction, locked for the diversionary route. The old line was abandoned except for a portion of the southbound line which was signalled as a reversing siding, although the access points and signal box were not brought into use just yet. Most of the old tracks were torn up to allow the formation to be rebuilt, and an old bridge near Northwood to be replaced, requiring temporary connections to be laid in to Northwood goods yard. At Northwood itself, because of site restrictions, the formation could only be widened on the east side so the existing tracks through the station were already in the right place to be on the future 'main' lines. In consequence it was only necessary to cut and slew the platform track to meet the new lines just south of the station. The second stage took place on 23rd April when the new 'main' tracks were commissioned between Northwood and Watford South Junction. At both these locations the tracks were already in the correct position so it was simply a matter of slewing the connections across at each end and abandoning the old lines. This changeover required the prior completion of one of the two new island platforms at Moor Park and the abandonment for demolition of the old wooden station, which was in the way of the second island.

The next stage saw the commissioning of the new main lines between Harrow North Junction and Northwood Hills. Amongst other things this involved the removal of the existing junction at Harrow North and the laying in of a new high-speed double junction, a very substantial piece of work completed over the weekend of 9th/10th September 1961, with new signalling commissioned from 11th September; commendably a train service was operated throughout this period. At this point the remainder of the double junction at Northwood Hills was commissioned, and the reversing siding and signal box brought into regular use. From 28th January 1962 the signalling on the old lines, now the 'local' roads, between North Harrow and Northwood Hills replaced the 1925 equipment. This move saw Pinner signal box closed, to be replaced by an interlocking machine operated from Harrow signal box, and really only intended for use during the time it was necessary to deal with goods trains in Pinner yard, although passenger trains could be reversed there.

The final stage of the 4-tracking work was completed and ready for traffic on 17th June 1962. This saw the new 'local' lines introduced between Northwood Hills and Watford South Junction. This complicated work involved the removal of the double-junction and siding at Northwood Hills and the complete relaying (again) of the trackwork at Watford South Junction. The new tracks (on the 'local' roads) passed through Northwood where a new southbound platform had been constructed and the old southbound one converted to an island with the new face serving northbound local trains; the former northbound platform was subsequently demolished, and the now-disused southbound face of the island soon obliterated by the construction of a new platform awning and screen wall. The commissioning work also required further alterations to the connections to Northwood Goods yard. The second island at Moor Park also came into service.

Signalling on the 4-track section was 3- or 4-aspect on the 'main' lines and 2-aspect on the local. As partially unbraked goods trains would operate on the local tracks it was thought desirable to provide some advanced warning of danger signals to goods drivers in the form of 'distant' signals; these were electro-pneumatically operated discs carrying a black fishtailed bar on a yellow ground (these were also provided on the tracks as far as Amersham). Although all the Underground trains and the new DMUs carried tripcocks, British Railways' expresses did not and it was felt prudent for the tracks upon which they would normally operate to have signals fitted with auxiliary red aspects; these were not illuminated unless the main red or yellow aspect failed, and in the case of a red aspect failure the preceding signal would also be kept at danger, giving advanced indication of trouble ahead. These auxiliary aspects are still in commission although all trains now carry tripcocks. The local lines were designed for maximum speeds of 60mph, and the main lines were laid out for 70mph running. Those between Rickmansworth and Aylesbury South had already been relaxed from 60mph to 70mph in October 1952; pre-War speed limits were 70mph from Harrow to Northwood Hills, 60mph to Chalfont, 70mph to Great Missenden and 75mph to Quainton Road, though there is much evidence for higher speeds being regularly achieved. Unfortunately, because of deteriorating track condition, a blanket 50mph speed restriction was imposed over the whole Met Line in 1989 which has only recently been relaxed.

The 4-tracking work caused various station alterations. North Harrow was least affected as the new line skirted the northbound platform; however the new bridge carrying the 'main' line required rebuilding of the western entrance in contemporary style and some changes within the ticket hall. Pinner was less fortunate as the new tracks meant demolishing the northbound platform buildings and their replacement by a new screen wall and awning; the southbound side was little altered except that a

The new station at Northwood is taking shape behind the hoardings where new platforms and tracks are being installed. The southbound platform canopy has already been partly demolished but that on the northbound platform remained until the platforms were replaced. The tracks in the foreground are now the fast lines and the platforms have been removed. The new station buildings are already in use and a temporary access bridge may be seen leading to the northbound platform. LT Museum

subway replaced the former footbridge (in 2003 a new footbridge superseded this subway). Northwood Hills required very little alteration as the buildings were already on the over line bridge and clear of the new tracks. At Northwood a completely new station was required, very much in the 1960s style of light brick and substantial glazing; the new station was on the bridge on the main road, replacing the old buildings in the approach road. As part of the works provision was made for electric trains to be able to reverse in either direction and the goods reception road was electrified so it could be used as a siding – this was intended for a possible Watford–Northwood shuttle but this was never introduced. The signalling at Northwood was controlled from a new interlocking machine operated from the push button panel at Harrow. Moor Park received a smart modern ticket hall handy for the select estate, and a new car park. A subway led to the new island platforms, and to an eastern exit and a heavily wooded footpath vaguely pointing towards Bushey (this was the side upon which the original entrance had been, but later arrival of housing on the other side had shifted the focus).

Prior to the inauguration of the extended electric services the Baker Street 8am – 9am peak hour comprised 29 arrivals in all, of which: 12 trains originated from Uxbridge, three from Aylesbury, one from Chesham, seven from Watford, five from Harrow, and one from Rickmansworth; these were supplemented by two trains running between Aylesbury and Marylebone. As just mentioned, it was not until 4-tracking got to Northwood Hills that anything much changed. The timetable introduced on 11th September 1961 continued to see 29 peak hour arrivals running in exactly the same pattern as before excepting only that the three Aylesbury trains had been cut back to Amersham and four out of the five Harrow trains now originated at Northwood Hills. New British Railways diesel multiple units now shuttled between Aylesbury and Amersham to make connections into the LT trains. The Aylesbury–Marylebone through trains continued uninterrupted. Off-peak Amersham to Baker Street trains operated at various intervals to fit in with the various British Railways offerings (some of which were now diesel units), but each LT train connected with a diesel shuttle.

Completion of the 4-tracking allowed the additional capacity to be exploited as well as a speeding up of overall journey time. The new timetable of 18th June 1962 saw the peak hour pattern offer a total of 27 trains arriving at Baker Street: 12 trains originated from Uxbridge, six from Amersham, one from Chesham, and eight from Watford; from this it will be seen that most of the additional Amersham trains were gained by extending trains previously short-worked. Just as importantly, four LMR trains from Aylesbury to Marylebone worked through during the same period. Off-peak an hourly Aylesbury–Marylebone service operated, running fast between Chorleywood and Harrow, and a half-hour Amersham–Baker Street service running fast between Moor Park and Harrow, thence fast to Finchley Road. Four trains an hour ran all stations to Baker Street from both Watford and Uxbridge.

Peak services were complicated by the range of non-stopping possibilities. Trains from Amersham either ran all stations or ran fast from Moor Park to Finchley Road (through Chesham trains always ran 'fast'). Trains from Watford or Uxbridge either ran all stations, or ran semi-fast, which meant non-stop from North Harrow to Finchley Road or Rayners Lane to Finchley Road, as the case may be. Perhaps confusingly the LMR fast trains omitted Rickmansworth and Moor Park, but did call at Harrow.

Scheduled journey times improved for a while. In 1959 the fastest journeys to Baker Street (arriving between 8am and 9am) were: 1hr 21mins from Aylesbury (and 50mins from Amersham), 41mins from Watford and 36mins from Uxbridge. The equivalent times in 1963 were respectively: 1hr 9mins (41mins), 36½mins and 35mins; the

Aylesbury timing allows for a change at Amersham. Probably most dramatic were the improvements in the Aylesbury–Marylebone run that reduced from 1hr 24mins to 59mins. First class accommodation was now available again on all trains.

Since LT trains no longer operated beyond Amersham the stations, track and the staff on the remainder of the line to Aylesbury South Junction were transferred to the British Railways London Midland Region from one minute after midnight on 11th September 1962. The boundary was fixed at a point '1000 yards north of signal RJW1, north of Amersham', which is just over 1¼ miles to the north. LT continued for a while to deal with track maintenance and other civil engineering as agents of the LMR, but in due course all matters relating to that section of line were taken over.

Significantly, the organisation of London Transport itself also changed during this period. In 1963 the British Transport Commission was abolished and LT became a nationalised industry, reporting directly to the Minister of Transport. A new British Railways Board (soon styled British Rail) and various ad hoc bodies were established to promote co-ordination between the two industries in the absence of an overarching organisation.

While the modernisation work was in hand the time came for the old signalling at Watford to be replaced, this still used the mechanical frame installed during 1925. This time London Transport's most recent labour-saving device was employed – the programme machine. This was a device upon which the daily timetable was encoded by means of rows of punched holes in a long plastic role; for each train movement the role was stepped forward and the position of the holes was decoded to set up the required routeing automatically, an air-operated interlocking machine being used as the interface between the control circuitry and the safety-critical signalling circuits. Two programme machines were provided at Watford, one controlling the sequence of trains and the other their departure times. Since the train service might easily deviate from the timetable some means of human intervention was needed and supervisory facilities were installed in Rickmansworth cabin. From here it was possible to cancel or insert extra trains in the programme sequence, or to operate the site manually by means of push button control, a special push button panel being provided for the purpose. If things were seriously out of hand Watford could be switched into an automatic reversing mode where trains were routed alternately into each platform with the route south cleared after four minutes. The new arrangements were commissioned from 29th September 1958.

The new train services required new trains, but it would be as well first to take stock of what was already operating. After the war the ex-Met MW compartment stock became more familiarly known by the new London Transport code of T Stock, and this predominantly operated the train services on the Watford branch together with occasional workings to London from Rickmansworth or Harrow; the use of such compartment stock on the former joint line was regarded as important. The Uxbridge branch was mainly operated by P Stock but following a reallocation of trains in the early 1950s just over half of the P Stock service was run by another type of train, the F Stock of 1920 origin, released by the District Line; this had three pairs of air-operated doors per car side and loaded and unloaded very quickly (handy at dealing with Wembley football crowds) though it might not have been regarded by everyone as entirely suitable for long journeys. The Aylesbury trains were still operated by 1910-design compartment stock hauled by electric locomotives south of Rickmansworth, and steam hauled to the north by Eastern Region (later London Midland Region) locomotives. The 1960 timetable required seventeen T Stock trains (of which eight were 8-coach and nine were 6-coach), eight F Stock trains (all 8-car), sixteen P Stock trains (of which

A southbound T Stock train awaits departure from Rickmansworth in the mid 1950s. The leading car is a steel-panelled motor car of 1931 origin. The new signalbox is just visible in the background. Don Jones

seven were 8-car and nine were 6-car), nine loco hauled trains (all 6-carriage), and the Chesham shuttle, still operated by three carriages of Victorian bogie stock arranged for 'push-pull' working. Unnecessary car mileage was kept to a minimum by operating the 6-vehicle trains off peak and where possible stabling the longer trains.

It was intended to replace the entire fleet of trains by one new class of rolling stock, the design of which LT agonised over for some years. The Met's passengers were influential and they strongly liked compartment stock. Significantly, compartments did offer the maximum seating area (important on the longer journeys) and boarding times were fast because of the number of doors and the agility of the regular travellers. The concern was that compartments were inconvenient for the standing passenger and they did not allow a load to distribute itself evenly. Furthermore, the use of swing doors was regarded as both a safety risk and a general inconvenience at the busy tunnel stations, and the construction of stock with isolated compartments was increasingly regarded as anachronistic. Those passengers who didn't like them, perhaps on public safety grounds, were equally vocal on the matter. It therefore looked as though any universal stock would be something of a compromise, and much effort was put into upsetting only the smallest number of people.

Mock-ups undertaken pre-war offered some ingenious suggestions as to how compartment-style seating could be combined with air-operated sliding doors but these ideas, which helped develop the thinking, were not pursued. Further ideas were developed during 1944/5 and resulted in a new mock-up design. This would have a wide body profile and three pairs of doors per car side and was to be divided up into three sections each containing a number of bays of facing seats. The bays seated three facing each way, with a gangway running along each side linking the bays together; one of the of the gangways also linked each section together, the section being divided by a floor to ceiling screen. A swing door would separate the sections and the 57 seats were to be of high-back profile over which would be supported traditional briefcase (or hat) racks. An experimental car entered service in January 1946 to gauge public reaction. The format followed the mock up closely except the section doors were omitted and the seats were only low-profile. The public reported a dislike of the layout, partly because, owing to the gangways, virtually no seats abutted any of the windows.

A second car to similar profile entered service in June 1947, this time with two doorways per car side, and with seating (totalling 56) in the more usual arrangement of facing pairs and of high-back profile. Significantly, glazed partitions divided the car into a number of smaller areas offering some concession to intimacy and helping to reduce draughts. From 2nd November 1949 the lessons learned thus far were presented to the public in a third experimental offering in the form of the first car with a completely new interior. This time it was found possible to dispose the seating in facing bays either side of an offset gangway which allowed 3-per-side seating on one side and 2-per-side on the other. Each pair of bays was separated from the door space by a glazed screen. This formula (which omitted luggage racks) was considered to offer a reasonable compromise in all the circumstances; this and the previous car ran until 1953. Other ideas were tested and mock-ups were even built, but in essence the 1949 prototype car was the starting point for the new fleet of trains, to be known as the 'A' stock.

In 1959 orders were placed with Cravens Ltd for the construction of 248 cars of new stock for the Metropolitan Line modernisation, equivalent to thirty-one 8-car trains. They were to be arranged in identical 4-car units each comprising a driving motor car at the outer ends and a pair of trailers in between. The units were to be capable of operation as 4-car trains during the off-peak periods and (unusually in LT practice) to be fully reversible so in the event that they were turned end for end by the triangular Watford junctions they could still couple together; automatic couplings were to be fitted at the outer ends of the units with intermediate cars semi-permanently coupled. The design followed quite closely the general layout of the 1949 prototype car with 3 + 2 high-backed seating and glazed screens at the doorways. By this means a seat width of 17½ inches per person was possible, described by LT at the time as 'adequate' and allowing an extra 80 seats per train more than would have been possible if 21-inch seats (in 2 + 2 formation) had been provided; the driving motors had 54 seats plus 4 tip-ups, and the trailers 58. The interior finishings had been improved with extensive use of grey fibreglass partitions and maroon melamine panelling, painted surfaces were grey. Importantly, the luggage racks had reappeared together (as an afterthought) with umbrella hooks.

Aluminium alloy had been used for several years on new LT rolling stock, and the emergence of A Stock with unpainted aluminium alloy exterior panelling was hardly a surprise. New features were the use of light alloy extrusions in some of the vertical structural members, such as the door pillars, and these also presented an external surface (these always stood out as a slightly different texture or shade). Deep section aluminium alloy underframes were also used in contrast to the usual steel, and special precautions were taken (in the form of 'crumple' zones) to prevent serious damage arising from the inevitable minor collisions that constantly arose, mainly in depots; these were subsequently judged as quite a success. Nevertheless more serious damage did arise on occasions and required the development of new techniques for the repair of aluminium components.

An 8-car train of F Stock passes a P Stock train approaching Eastcote on the Uxbridge line in the 1950s. The F Stock had only a short life on the Metropolitan.

Below Neasden Yard in October 1958 with an 8-car P Stock train in the foreground.

Bottom A nearly new A Stock train at Harrow-on-the-Hill. The unpainted aluminium alloy finish kept in good condition for about ten years, but visually failed the test of time.

At 9ft 8ins, each carriage was built to the maximum width possible in the tunnel sections, and they remain the widest trains in use on the Underground: at 53ft they were then also the longest (the trains are still the longest but individual cars are no longer so). While the trailers were very similar to the 1949 prototype car the motor cars were necessarily different as they had to accommodate a position for the guard at the trailing end; these therefore had a single door at that position and two pairs of double doors per car side. The electrical equipment was of the then standard camshaft design but this time supplying the four traction motors on each motor car, the motors being 300 volt machines arranged on each bogie as a pair permanently coupled in series (the first time this had been done on production trains). The stock was fitted with a switch which altered the electrical characteristics from slow acceleration/high speed for operation north of Finchley Road, and high acceleration/lower speed for operation in the tunnel sections where, apart from anything else, the trains needed to be in tune with other trains operating on the Circle Line. At its higher setting the trains were designed for a maximum speed of 60mph, though they could go faster downhill!

The first of the new trains was delivered to the Underground in February 1961 and entered service on 12th June, with 16 in service by the end of the year; this addressed the whole of the Amersham and Chesham service and had made a start on the replacement of the T Stock on the Watford line. By this time the original order had been supplemented by a further 27 trains which would allow the scrapping of the F Stock on the Uxbridge line and the transfer of the P Stock to the District. The original batch was styled the A60 Stock, and the second batch A62, though they were for all practical purposes identical. The last T Stock train operated on 5th October 1962, on a run from Watford just after the evening rush hour. The deliveries of A62 Stock began in mid-1962, with 12 trains in service by the end of that year, but it wasn't until March 1963 that the last F Stock train ran. The final A Stock train entered service in December 1963. There were some teething troubles with insufficiently tested methods such as the static converters which supplied the emergency lights and required subsequent fitting of tungsten emergency lamps at doorways. The emergence of stress fractures in the bogie frames had also to be addressed quickly, with comparative success.

Overall, though, the new trains were considerably more reliable than the ones they replaced, and this greatly expedited the inauguration of the new services. Nor were they probably an unreasonable design compromise, though the paying customers were understandably unhappy about the reduction in seating from the 600 of a T Stock train to 464 of A Stock. The vociferous and influential passengers from the outer reaches were not concerned that the amount of standing space had been increased considerably as it was not their habit to stand. They didn't understand that the A Stock had to be fitted with through gangways to meet regulations for working in the Finchley Road tunnels, and that standing capacity was essential for work over the Circle Line, or any of the other issues which made the trains the compromise necessary when outer and inner suburban (or Metro) services interwork.

There were some questions about the ride quality of the A Stock which, even in early days, had come to note with observations of serious 'pitching' at speed, partly resolved on later cars which were delivered with one of the suspension components inverted to change the pitching axis. Nevertheless the ride remains both indifferent and very variable. However as the T Stock has been seen described as 'a cocktail shaker on wheels' the newer trains were still perhaps an improvement even if the seats were a little firmer. Relevant here is the inevitable comparison passengers made (and make) with the diesel multiple units (DMUs) on the Aylesbury service.

The transformation of the Met – a loco-hauled northbound train of T Stock approaching Rickmansworth passes new A Stock in the sidings awaiting use.

Class 5 4-6-0 No. 45292 with a train from Marylebone to Nottingham passing Chorleywood on 3rd September 1966, the last day of through trains over the former Great Central main line. F.W. Goudie

In the final days of steam operation on the Metropolitan Line this view at Rickmansworth shows the steam engine that has just come off the southbound train running back towards the steam lay -by sidings at the north end of the station, while its replacement electric loco backs onto the train. LT Museum

The existing steam trains would have been little match for the A Stock but the new DMUs were another matter. Quickly introduced during 1960/61 the new trains were 4-coach Derby-built sets each comprising a pair of (brake) second-class driving motors, a second class trailer and a composite trailer; total seating was 312 of which 30 were first class. The composite coaches also carried lavatories. Sufficient cars were built to make up forty 4-coach (or twenty 8-coach) trains with some odd vehicles left for the spares pool; the units operated on all services from Marylebone, not just the Amersham–Aylesbury route. The relative comfort compared with A Stock, lavatories, the existence of first class, the limited stopping and doors which were only open for as long as it took people to use them (and fierce heating in winter) made them appear more comfortable than A Stock and north of Rickmansworth their use picked up quickly. By 1966 most of the peak hour 4-coach trains had been lengthened to eight, and they were becoming busy.

The ability of the 8-car A Stock trains to uncouple was soon put to use. It was natural to want to avoid hauling around under-utilised carriages unnecessarily and the Metropolitan Railway had made a practice of running shorter trains off peak either by uncoupling surplus carriages or dividing long trains into shorter ones. This practice had died out by the war and had not been re-introduced. Once A Stock predominated it was possible to reintroduce off peak uncoupling and from the June 1962 timetable 4-car trains were run. Trains were normally scheduled to couple and uncouple at Watford and Uxbridge in the platforms, and at Amersham in the sidings. In most cases one long train split into two short ones (or vice versa during coupling) but sometimes one portion was stabled. Introduction of uncoupling on the Met coincided with its withdrawal everywhere else on the Underground as having proved a considerable operational irritation with questionable benefits, but the environment of the Met was a little different. It did require signalling alterations at Watford where 'calling-on' signals were needed to allow trains to enter partly occupied platforms (such facilities already existed at Uxbridge); coupling and uncoupling at Watford was thenceforth controlled by programme machine.

With the new services it was concluded that additional sidings were required at Rickmansworth, which was a convenient point to handle stabling requirements for both Amersham and Watford (via the north curve). Five new sidings were built to the south of the station on the north side of the line, extending nearly as far as Watford North Junction; two sidings came into use on 28th May 1961, and the remainder on 11th June.

The three locomotive sidings at Rickmansworth (two steam and one electric) were formally decommissioned from 16th September 1961 as they were no longer needed. From 25th September 1961 other alterations at Rickmansworth meant the bay platform used for the Watford shuttle service was no longer available for passenger trains, but during the winter was often used to keep a 'sleet' locomotive comprising two of the old T Stock cars to which tanks of de-icing fluid were fitted and from which the fluid could be sprayed onto the conductor rails to discourage ice formation.

It is perhaps unfortunate that the copious infrastructure finished in 1962 was only briefly, if ever, used to anything like its capacity as several intended purposes soon disappeared. The first eventuality was the closure of what was still called the Great Central main line, which happened in two stages. Although under Eastern Region control the main line enjoyed a mild revival and supported two named express trains (the *South Yorkshireman* and the *Master Cutler*, both of which ran over the Met section) their immediate withdrawal when the LMR took over in 1958 put down an ominous marker. During this period the viability of the local services north of Aylesbury was questioned; these were broadly the services that either originated from Woodford Halse or Brackley, or long distance trains which called at some or all local stations (by 1960 the combined service from north of Aylesbury to the Metropolitan Line had dwindled to only seven trains a day). The decision was taken that local stations north of Aylesbury should be closed with effect from 4th March 1963, including Quainton Road, which was last served on 2nd March, as there was no Sunday service. Local trains were either withdrawn or cut back to Aylesbury, and the long distance trains just non-stopped former local stations.

The new station building at Moor Park opened on 23rd April 1961. LT Museum

The second stage of closure resulted from the so-called 'Beeching' report of April 1963 which had identified the ex-GC line as one from which passenger services should be withdrawn completely. It was difficult to defend a route never used to capacity, which provided few through services not possible by some other means, and which had just abandoned its local trains. Nevertheless, even in 1961, there were still five weekday trains a day from Nottingham which all stopped at Harrow-on-the-Hill (one of which called all stations except Northwood Hills and North Harrow) and an overnight from Liverpool; by 1965 the equivalent trains now all ran fast south of Aylesbury though a couple still called at Harrow. With the death warrant signed, the last main line passenger train operated on 3rd September 1966, from which time no scheduled passenger trains operated further north than Aylesbury. Track lifting on the GC main line began in 1968 but a single line was retained between Aylesbury and the wartime spur at Calvert for special non-passenger workings. The station buildings at Quainton Road remain, but are now in the hands of a preservation group. Together this meant the end of loco-hauled main line trains on the Met.

Also run into oblivion was the British Railways pick-up freight business, initially through a regime of concentration in key rail yards and onward distribution by road, and then letting the whole business go. All this resulted in a rapid rundown of freight business on the Met and the closure of all the freight yards, most of which ended up as car parks or property development sites. Transfer of goods responsibility to the LNER had already seen off transfer movements via Finchley Road from 1948 (in favour of Neasden LNER) with local goods traffic no longer running south of Willesden Green from 1955, but for a while all the other local yards thrived. British Railways refused to serve Willesden Green which meant that in its last years LT had to run its own goods train each day between Willesden and Neasden goods yards, generally using its ageing Peckett 0-6-0 saddle tank locomotive. Goods services on the Uxbridge branch ceased in 1964 and all the yards were closed. Most of the yards on the Willesden Green–Quainton Road section closed in 1966 (including Watford and Croxley), and the larger yards at Pinner and Harrow closed in 1967. With the withdrawal of freight the distant signals disks were no longer needed and were soon decommissioned, though some of the posts and mechanisms remained for years. Closure of the goods yards also meant some interlockings (sometimes still old signal boxes) were no longer required and they were removed with signals converted for automatic working; this even extended to the new IMR at Pinner in 1970, decommissioned after only eight years use, though Northwood was retained as an emergency reversing point. It may also be noted that between 1965 and 1967 parcels facilities were also withdrawn from the former joint line stations (the huge parcels depot at Harrow became the Underground's ticket sorting office until the futility of ticket sorting became evident twenty years later), though carriage of newspapers continued until the early 1970s, notably on Metropolitan Line trains from Baker Street where they were usually carried in the guard's section.

The impact of this could have been very much more severe. At the time of the British Railways takeover north of Amersham the train services had been operating at a heavy loss, and the planned closure of all services to the north would not make it any easier for the Marylebone–Aylesbury services to be financially viable. In addition Marylebone became heavily under-utilised and represented prime development land. In the mood of the moment, in those difficult days of 1963 when lines were fighting for survival, services to even a large town like Aylesbury looked threatened notwithstanding the brand new trains and vastly accelerated timetable. Informally LT was asked for a view; such a line would not be allowed to close without 'adequate' replacement services. The speculation was that Aylesbury itself could continue to be served from the old Wycombe Railway line to Princes Risborough (still single track) whose trains could be diverted to Paddington. The journey would inevitably have been much longer. In terms of dealing with intermediate stations (Great Missenden and Wendover – traffic to Stoke Mandeville was negligible) options were to get people to railhead to Amersham (using buses if possible), or extending electrification to Great Missenden or Wendover. LT thought Great Missenden a possibility, especially as it was comparatively busy, but judged Wendover very expensive. Under the 1962 Transport Act LT no longer had powers to run rail services beyond Amersham, which was at the very edge of its territory, although that could have been altered. Fortunately as the year went on it became obvious that traffic on the rejuvenated service was rising rapidly and showed every likelihood in due course of breaking even. Furthermore LT's planning forecasts suggested that within a few years the numbers of people living in the Met's territory would make it impossible to handle everyone on the services south of Harrow-on-the-Hill without augmentation from services into Marylebone. The issue subsided, but only for a while, and we shall return to the matter again.

With electrification at the north end of the Met, and various other enhancements (not least the impending Victoria Line), LT's thirst for power was constantly rising. In London Transport hands Neasden power station received some early modernisation but its fate was really sealed during the war and the changed circumstances thereafter. LT originally wanted Neasden to support the New Works Programme, and it was hoped to begin standardising distribution frequency at 50 cycles rather than $33\frac{1}{3}$. Neasden produced only the latter but plans were put in place for gradual conversion. After preliminary work (which included taking 50-cycle supplies from East London mainly as a back up) work stopped during the War and Neasden only ever produced the lower frequency.

With the exception of partial conversion to oil firing (mainly in 1947/8), and abandonment of the dried up wells, little else changed; at its peak Neasden's capacity rose to 89.7MW, but was always the smallest of LT's three power houses. With the station getting desperately old by the late 1950s the decision was made not to re-equip the station but instead to take a bulk supply from the national grid. An intake and associated switch house were constructed in 1963 and over the following five years the various substations served by Neasden were altered to 50 cycle operation and the old power station's load reduced accordingly. It finally shut down on 21st July 1968, by which time it was the last $33\frac{1}{3}$ cycle power station in the country. Demolition of this massive building took place mainly the following year, the end of a major landmark.

Worth mentioning here is Neasden's need to get rid of vast quantities of ash and other waste. One solution was to dump it on spare land and dedicated tip sidings were built for this purpose. The first dump was at Rayners Lane in the angle of the junction; these sidings came into use in 1912 and were retained until 1955 by which time the ground level (upon which there are now houses) was raised by about fifteen feet. The tip was replaced by a new one (called Croxley tip) by the Grand Union Canal near Watford South Junction, on the site of gravel workings which had been connected with the Met many years previously. Inevitably much of LT's general rubbish also got dumped here and the sidings remained in regular use until the 1980s. Croxley tip trains were steam-hauled by ex-GWR pannier tank locomotives (bought by LT in the 1960s) until 1971 following which pairs of battery locomotives were used.

Recent times

In 1970 most of the London Transport organisation was transferred to the Greater London Council (formed in 1965), where it stayed until 1984 whence it returned to government control. In 1985 the Underground assets and operations were established as a limited company (London Underground Limited), continuing to report to the parent body, now renamed London Regional Transport (or London Transport for short). In 1988, the Metropolitan Line was established as a distinct management unit within the Underground, having a large measure of day-to-day responsibility for service provision and in due course for most routine maintenance. This has all changed again. In anticipation of the Underground's transfer to 'Transport for London', an executive arm of the new Greater London Authority, and of other structural changes to the engineering functions, day to day control of the Met is now in the hands of a management group controlling all the sub-surface lines, though still a part of London Underground Ltd. The 1988 reorganisation did trigger the launch of the Hammersmith & City service in its own colour (salmon pink) from 1990, thus ending the fiction that these services were somehow part of the same Metropolitan Line that worked the services north of Baker Street. Of course the Metropolitan Line still had to be shown in parallel from Baker Street to Aldgate, but it made things much clearer. At the end of the day managements come and go, and will doubtless continue to do so, but structural changes really affect the bidding for and prioritisation of funding and it is now worth looking at the more recent impact of such expenditure.

Of major significance were the opening of the Jubilee Line on 1st May 1979 between Baker Street and Charing Cross, and the transfer of the Bakerloo Line Stanmore branch to the new line, producing a through route from Stanmore to Charing Cross. There was at first little impact on the parallel Metropolitan Line services, but over the years separation of staffing, management and operating practices conspired to eliminate the inter-operation of Metropolitan Line trains over the slow, now Jubilee, tracks for some empty workings which took place early or late in the traffic day and in emergencies.

Of the more pressing objectives of London Underground was the replacement of the worn out signalling, much of which was of pre-war origin; the Metropolitan Line north of Baker Street was especially rich in such equipment. Before discussing general signal replacement it is a convenient point to mention the proximity of Ruislip depot on the Central Line, which lies just to the south of the Met between Ruislip and Ickenham but had not historically had any reason for physical interconnection. However Ruislip was under-utilised and had become the main commissioning depot for new trains as well as a major track refurbishment establishment with need for better access to the network. From 28th September 1975 an electrified connection was made via a new reversing siding on the south side of the Metropolitan Line. Controlled from Rayners Lane signal box, it provided access to Ruislip depot and could also be used for reversing Metropolitan and Piccadilly trains terminating at Ruislip, enabling the old mechanical (but seldom used) signal box there to be closed, the last such box on the Met.

In 1974 London Transport made an early foray into computerised signalling when a minicomputer was installed at Watford, where it temporarily took over control from the programme machines until it was moved to Heathrow Central. The computer, minute by modern standards, proved quite robust and started more serious development work on computer controlled signalling.

The signalling between Baker Street and Canons Park was completely modernised during 1984–85, replacing that installed between 1937 and 1954. At reversing points and junctions new remotely controlled interlocking machines were provided although control itself was retained by signalmen in the existing signal cabins; the signal frame at Finchley Road was superseded by a temporary push-button control panel, but at Willesden Green the existing frame, and at Wembley Park the existing control desk, were temporarily adapted.

The re-signalling was a prelude to the transfer of local control to a new integrated computerised control centre at Baker Street, which would eventually supervise all train movements between Aldgate and Wembley Park on the Metropolitan Line, and Charing Cross and Stanmore on the Jubilee. The control room opened on 25th October 1986, with operation of the Stanmore interlocking transferred to the new facility. Charing Cross–Baker Street followed on 30th November 1986 with control transferred from the signal box at Finchley Road. West Hampstead and Finchley Road itself were transferred on 18th January 1987 with Willesden Green following on 1st February 1987 and Wembley Park signal box on 12th April 1987, completing this phase of the exercise.

For another year the signal boxes at Neasden (North and South) were retained to control movements to and from the depot. From 16th October 1988 these were replaced by a depot control room that controlled all train movements within the depot, ground signals and track circuits having been universally provided outside the sheds, and the points motorised. Computerised 'solid state' interlocking was installed, intended as much as anything else to test on a comprehensive scale its reliability prior to further possible use on the Underground.

Baker Street signal box dated back to 1924 but the equipment wasn't superseded until July 1987 when a new interlocking machine room came into operation together with a modified track layout that increased the berth in platform 1. The signalling remained physically controlled from the old signal box via a new push button panel until it was transferred to the new control centre the following year.

Probably the project causing the most change to the public's perception of the Met was the huge amount of work undertaken from the end of 1986 to install the new systemwide Underground Ticketing System (UTS), involving computerised ticket issuing with encoded tickets which could be read electronically. Key by-products of this were the universal provision of new high-security ticket offices equipped with windows for manual service and prominent passenger operated ticket machines that could be serviced from within the ticket office area. At first the only stations to be equipped with automatic ticket gates to check all tickets on entry to and exit from the system were installed in central London. At outer stations (all those north of Baker Street) manual checking continued. The concept was that outside 'Zone 1' tickets would be checked on a random basis with penalty fares charged if passengers were caught without a valid travel document.

All this meant the sweeping away of all the old-fashioned ticket offices, and this had a significant impact on the appearance of many stations. Included in the project were the freestanding booths known as 'Passimeters' that characterise in particular the

A 4-car train of A Stock at Northwood Hills in August 1980, the last summer of operation of single units in off-peaks. Brian Hardy

Holden stations, such as those on the Uxbridge branch. Many original and little-changed Metropolitan Railway ticket offices disappeared during this process, or at least were vastly modified. In the late 1990s, as part of a private finance initiative programme, ticket gating was extended to all stations; however, as provision had been made in the initial UTS station design for this eventuality the impact was less profound.

Many other stations have been upgraded during the last thirty years or so, though in most cases the effect has been to restore them to a consistent standard. Baker Street itself has been the victim of a large number of important works but the impact on the Met main platforms has been unfortunate, with the 1912 finishes in poor condition and a multiplicity of expedient in-filling and arbitrary finishes (or no finishes) at platform level ruining what was once the Met's pride and joy. The ticket hall has received more sensitive treatment though the station exterior still awaits a caring eye. The wooden platforms and booking hut at West Harrow survived until 1989 when the station was comprehensively rebuilt with (slightly) more modern facilities, the updated station being completed in late 1990. At about the same time road improvements at Hillingdon required bodily movement of the station, which was in the way of the upgraded A40. Since the old station was another wooden affair this well suited London Underground who would get funding for the works, resulting in a substantial new structure clad in glass and white enamelled-iron panels. The new station was eventually completed during late 1993 having been shunted towards Uxbridge by about half a train's length.

The operation of short trains during the summer off-peak, with uncoupling in service, had been abandoned after the 1980 summer as it had become an operational nuisance no longer possible to justify (uncoupling was in any case always cancelled during each winter as it was hazardous during leaf-fall and icy conditions). This was greatly to simplify subsequent rolling stock modifications.

From 29th September 1986 one-person operation was introduced on the Met. For this to happen considerable alterations were required to the rolling stock so that door controls could be located in the driving cabs and much new safety equipment added. Without regular uncoupling of units it was felt not worthwhile to fit the new equipment in all cabs, as some cabs could be permanently confined to the middle of trains. The outcome was the creation of units that could only work at either the north or the south end of trains, with some double-ended units. The need to rewire the trains also meant loss of unit reversibility. Both these factors meant a reduction of flexibility of the trains, but the high number of spare units was felt sufficient to cope.

The A Stock has proved decidedly robust; this being so, the question arose as to when it should be replaced, a matter usually decided by a combination of unreliability, structural degradation, rising maintenance expense, and obsolescence of design. Matters were influenced by an urgent need to review the interior finishings of the trains which, although not having given rise to a problem, no longer conformed to latest safety standards. The view was that with a refitted interior the car bodies were good for another 10–15 years use and despite their age this appeared to be a worthwhile approach. During 1989 two units were fitted with different interiors to gauge public reaction, and the trains were also painted in the new LUL corporate livery, considerably enhancing their appearance; by this time the unpainted aluminium exteriors had begun to look very poor and had further suffered from extensive graffiti damage (graffiti had badly affected all aspects of the Metropolitan Line at around that time). The outcome was a considered design that was applied to the entire fleet between 1994 and 1997, and included the fitting of end windows to improve passenger security.

A Stock cars being refurbished, showing the new end windows installed in the trailer cars. The interiors were further brightened in 2003 by the fitting of a new design of seat moquette. Les Collings

The value to British Rail of the land at Marylebone kept beckoning, and the higher the property value became the more it beckoned. Furthermore, during the early 1980s traffic levels using the remaining services into Marylebone were declining, and those on the parallel Metropolitan Line had stabilised at a point where they were only running 24 trains an hour into Baker Street, instead of 28 which was judged to be the practical limit following resignalling. In addition, a government-sponsored report into the possibility of conversion of certain roads into railways had just been undertaken and of the few routes which appeared to be viable was one from Northolt to Marylebone. British Rail went for it, and the closure notice was issued on 15th March 1984. Since British Rail had been working up to this, Marylebone had already acquired that air of dereliction and decay that presages closure.

LT's view was that the transfer of traffic to the Underground could just about be accommodated. A factor in all this was the debacle of the Greater London Council's 'Fare's Fare' campaign which had seen a general reduction of fares, followed by a court case which had then resulted in the fares doubling (with significant reductions in train services), followed by a further fares reduction but not yet any compensating train service increases. It was about the only period when LT could apparently handle the additional traffic caused by Marylebone's closure.

Proceedings got under way and took some ugly turns. Intriguingly the closure process was arrested by a sudden announcement on 30th April 1986 that Marylebone would remain open. It was hinted darkly that traffic levels on the Underground had gone up so much (15 per cent) since closure was announced that it was impossible to divert Marylebone traffic to the Underground. Perhaps more relevant was the dawn of a positive marketing campaign for Marylebone services during 1985 under the 'Chiltern Line' brand which had shown immediate prospects for traffic growth. The emergence of a new management structure at the end of 1985 (which later flowered as Network SouthEast) would certainly have had a major influence on events.

With signalling and rolling stock at the end of their lives, and Marylebone very run down, British Rail now embarked upon a programme of investment which saw Marylebone massively refurbished, new signalling and upgraded track, and early delivery of new turbo diesels with much improved levels of comfort and better performance. The new trains entered service from 1991 in mainly 2-coach or 3-coach formations, though these could be coupled together to form longer trains. LUL took the opportunity to insist that any of these operating over the Met Line would be required to have tripcocks fitted and operational. As the popularity of the Chiltern service grew rapidly, timetables were soon enhanced and longer trains came into operation during peak hours. Singled out as an early privatisation candidate the new owners have continued to innovate, with certain services over the Metropolitan Line operating non-stop in order to relieve loadings on other trains.

It would not be fruitful to track every single change to Met timetables over recent years, but the highlights need recording. Initially train services from 1962 remained comparatively stable, though the BR DMUs began to call at Rickmansworth and Moor Park during the off peaks. From 1968 a serious staff shortage (caused in part by migration of traincrews to the Victoria Line, and by poor general pay and conditions) required some thinning down of services, achieved by withdrawing specific services which created unfortunate gaps. Other trains were cancelled in abundance on a day-to-day basis. Things improved slightly from January 1970, although the off-peak Amersham service was reduced to hourly (not actually much of a hardship as the cancelled train was the one immediately following a through BR DMU).

From 1975 train services were recast and the peak fast and semi fast trains began calling at Harrow-on-the-Hill (and at West Harrow, if they came from Uxbridge). This move at least partly originated from the staff shortages which were still evident and had caused passengers waiting an unduly long time at Harrow to complain about trains trundling through without stopping – quite possibly with some empty seats. This was to change permanently the habits of those living north or east of Harrow who would now seek to change there for a faster journey or a better connection. From then on the general pattern of peak timetable remained broadly unchanged until 2003 except for variations in the scheduling pattern to try and minimise mounting service unreliability. Over the last few years the formula has been to build in standing time at Harrow, especially for southbound trains, partly to try and offer connecting trains and partly to present trains at Wembley Park to time to minimise the queuing where the fast and slow tracks converge, a problem which has become endemic. From 1980 the all-stations peak trains to and from Amersham generally became semi-fast, at the expense of some trains (mainly on the Watford service) that became all-stations. In a further attempt to combat unreliability, from September 2003 all peak flow 'all stations' trains ran to or from Uxbridge, all 'semi-fast' trains to or from Watford and all 'fast' trains to or from Amersham. While this reduced conflicting paths at Harrow it profoundly reduced choice, especially for local journeys, and was the first time in over 80 years that the Uxbridge line has had only 'all-stations' trains.

A significant change to the rush hour service pattern to the City occurred from 26th January 1981 when the fast Amersham service was extended from Liverpool Street to Aldgate. Hitherto the view had been that Aldgate couldn't handle the entire Metropolitan Line service and just as the Aylesbury trains had reversed at Liverpool Street (which had retained the loco changing facilities after the war) then so must the fast Amersham/Chesham trains follow. The outcome was that Aldgate was found to be able to handle all the trains but that much smarter working was required if delays were not to occur. It took some time before the courage was found to withdraw the bay platform at Liverpool Street from use, but having done so Moorgate remained as a possible short working point for late running inbound trains. To improve (deteriorating) service reliability 'stepping back' was introduced at Aldgate during the peak hours from 28th September 1997; under this regime the operator who brings a train into one of the two reversing platforms at Aldgate takes out the following train from the same platform. This means that a departing train has an operator ready.

From 1982 peak intervals were lengthened in the light of a prevailing funding difficulty, but overall service patterns were retained. At this point it is worth recalling that the 1963 timetable required 52 x 8-car (and 1 x 4-car) trains in service utilising precisely the whole of the stock ordered if allowance is made for the 10 per cent spare stock for servicing; the 1982 timetable demanded only 39 x 8-car trains (and 1 x 4-cars), so services had drifted downwards from those offered at first, and much A Stock was sitting around spare allowing some units to be deployed on the East London Line.

Continuing unreliability caused peak reductions in 2002 with trains arriving at Baker Street cut from 25 to 21 in the busiest hour. The peak service pattern in 2003 might usefully be described so that comparison might be made with the information given earlier. In the 8am–9pm period (at Baker Street) the 21 arrivals comprise: seven from Watford, 11 from Uxbridge, one from Amersham and two from Chesham. Of all these, some 14 proceed through to the City. Fastest scheduled journey times (just increased) are: Amersham 45 mins, Watford 40 mins, Uxbridge 41 mins. The number of trains in peak service has increased to 44, including the Chesham shuttle. Significantly during this same period Chiltern Railways operate four DMUs to Marylebone, the fastest journey being achieved in 52 minutes from Aylesbury (31 minutes from Amersham and thence non stop).

Off-peak services have also been subject to significant changes. From the new timetable of 14th May 1990 all Amersham and Uxbridge trains were extended through to Aldgate during the midday and evening periods and at weekends, the first time ever this had been done. Despite some concerns at the time this form of operation proved immediately popular and was much welcomed as it avoided the awkward changes at Baker Street as well as the overcrowded trains running over the north side of the Circle Line. From May 1994 off-peak services were improved by increasing Uxbridge branch services from four to six trains an hour (all stations) with two of the existing Watford branch trains made semi-fast to Aldgate. This produced a complex train service pattern which did little for reliability. In an attempt to do something about it the May 2001 timetable simplified the service pattern with all Uxbridge trains working through to the City at 10-minute intervals, and Watford/Amersham trains reversing at Baker Street.

Watford Met station is very poorly situated indeed and has minimal usage. Equally the British Rail service to Croxley Green (built almost perversely with little object but to frustrate the Met's plans) never flowered and collapsed completely in 1996. Although the Metropolitan did consider extending to the High Street when circumstances allowed, it was never urgent and a bus did the job less expensively; the Met did buy some land in and behind the High Street that had become available in 1927 which might have formed the basis of a central station, but this was soon let to tenants and eventually passed to the Lewis Omnibus Company. This land found its way into London Transport and when in 1948 the question arose of what to do with it the issue was again raised of extension of the Watford branch to the town centre. The view then was that if a link to the town centre was desired then it could more effectively be achieved by linking with the British Railways line to Croxley Green, which also served the High Street. Over more recent years several studies have confirmed this view, including advanced feasibility studies. Such an extension would disadvantage very few people but would open up new transport links in the Watford area. The Metropolitan Line station would close and the line would be diverted a little to the south to meet the (presently closed) Croxley Green branch nearly head on.

On 15th July 2003 London Underground passed to the London Mayor's Transport for London organisation from the half-century old London Transport, which was abolished without ceremony. With improvements in public transport very much on the Mayor's agenda it will be interesting to see what changes are made, but early indications are that service volume, service reliability and passenger security feature as high priorities. The new public-private partners for the line are Metronet SSL (Sub Surface Lines). A programme of station refurbishment is being embarked upon and during the next decade Bombardier will be building a new fleet of trains. Current thinking is that there will be a common design, with through gangways, across all sub-surface lines – a serious challenge indeed to the compromises needed to address short distance journeys on the Circle Line and comparatively long distance journeys of more than 40 minutes on the Metropolitan where a seat and some peace are demanded from passengers, features more or less met at the moment. The Metropolitan, with its tight hold on Middlesex suburbia, is even today that little bit special and looks forward to another century of progress in the service it offers to London.